Crucial Moments

Stories of Support in Times of Crisis

Jeffrey T. Mitchell, Ph.D.
University of Maryland Baltimore County
Co-Founder of the
International Critical Incident Stress Foundation

William "Josey" L. Visnovske
Special Agent
Certified Fire Investigator,
Bureau of Alcohol, Tobacco, Firearms, and Explosives

Dedication

For my Father, Loren, and my Mother, Rita,
Who were my first crisis intervention instructors.
And to my children, Kyla and Angela "Annie,"
They are the loves of my life. They give me the energy to
reach way up high and achieve what I could not do without
them.

- Jeffrey T. Mitchell -

Dedication

For my family, who sacrifice their time with me while I try to help others find hope that the next day will be better than the day the trauma occurred. And for my friend Lee, who opened his heart to me and gave me a place where I can find peace in the sometime harsh realities of life.

- William "Josey" L. Visnovske -

About the Authors
Jeffrey T. Mitchell, Ph.D.

Jeffrey T. Mitchell, PhD is Clinical Professor of Emergency Health Services at the University of Maryland in Baltimore County, Maryland. He is a member of the Graduate Faculty of the University of Maryland. He is President Emeritus of the International Critical Incident Stress Foundation. He earned his Ph.D. in Human Development from the University of Maryland. After serving as firefighter/ paramedic for ten years, he developed a comprehensive, integrated, systematic, and multi-component crisis intervention program called "Critical Incident Stress Management."

He has authored over 250 articles and 16 books in the stress and crisis intervention fields. He serves as an adjunct faculty member of the Emergency Management Institute of the Federal Emergency Management Agency. He is a reviewer for the Journal of the American Medical Association (JAMA) and the International Journal of Emergency Mental Health. He received the Austrian Red Cross Bronze Medal for his work in Crisis Intervention in the aftermath of the Kaprum, Austria train tunnel fire. The Association of Traumatic Stress Specialists approved Dr. Mitchell as a Certified Trauma Specialist.

The United Nations appointed him to the United Nations Department of Safety and Security Working Group on Stress. He has consulted on stress, crisis, and trauma topics in 28 nations and in every one of the 50 United States.

William "Josey" L. Visnovske

William "Josey" Visnovske was born in the Midwest on a small farm to blue collar parents. At an early age he found the outdoors to be the place where he felt he most belonged.

Mr. Visnovske is a Certified Fire Investigator with the Bureau of Alcohol, Tobacco, Firearms, and Explosives. In his 25-year career, he has also served as a deputy sheriff, a city police officer, a state law enforcement officer, and a United States Marine. He served as an undercover officer for six years.

He is an International Critical Incident Stress Foundation approved instructor for the individual and group crisis intervention courses. He also volunteers as a specialized peer support team member at the On Site Academy in Massachusetts, a residential training and treatment facility for emergency and military personnel struggling with critical incident stress and Post Traumatic Stress Disorder. During the last five years, he has worked with Dr. Jeffrey T. Mitchell and conducted research into the psychological reactions of fire investigators, law enforcement, and fire service personnel who are exposed to fatality fire scenes. He was privileged to serve in a peer support role in the West Texas fire and explosion as well as in a multiple fire fatality situation in Charleston, W. V. He serves as a peer support member of ATF's Peer Response Program. He is a member of ATF's National Response Team.

At an early age he began to write short stories to process the events of his life, events that he witnessed. Story writing helped him to understand and clarify his own traumatic or unusual life experiences. He was surprised when friends suggested he publish a few of his stories in law enforcement journals. He did so with some degree of hesitation. To publish his work in a book was a huge step. It is hard for someone trained in undercover work to take on a public role. He had to be convinced by numerous conversations with Dr. Jeff Mitchell that contributing some of his stories to this book might help some people to find a way out of their pain and distress.

Table of Contents

INTRODUCTION

Things happen; people change. Most rebound and resume their lives. Some things, however, have a crushing effect and people may not be able to fully recover. Most people experience those awful moments now and then in their lives. These are crucial moments that sear the soul, fracture the heart, leave memories that cannot be eradicated, and wound and weaken the body. Accidents, severe illness, combat, the death of a child, a spouse, or a best friend, a divorce, the loss of a job or social status, and violence against one's person are but a few of the tragic events that can strike with little or no warning. They can influence the rest of our lives.

Not all crucial moments cause damage. Some crucial moments are opportunities for creativity, growth, and change and they can influence decisions and the acceptance of new challenges. Some crucial moments lead to progress, improvements for human societies, and better ways to care for each other. Sometimes crucial moments occur, but no one acts in the moment and an opportunity passes with neither a positive nor a negative outcome.

Crucial Moments is an unusual book. It is a mix of history, true stories, information, instructions, and guidance in the field of Critical Incident Stress Management (CISM). Each lesson is designed to provide insights into Crisis Intervention. Each chapter offers stories that illustrate the principles and practices of crisis support. The stories will enhance your understanding of peer support while they make you think. Some will certainly touch your heart.

1

Roadmap

Travel to all fifty states and to twenty-eight nations has taught me many valuable lessons. One important lesson is that roadmaps really help. Orientation, direction, pinpointing local attractions, and time estimates are among a number of benefits of a roadmap.

When "Josey" and I began discussing and planning this book we agreed that figurative roadmaps would help. We discussed the book's length, its structure, its timelines for completion, and the workload distribution. In essence, we developed a roadmap for the book.

We agreed to start off the book with a discussion of roadmaps for recovery. All too often people are traumatized when life and the circumstances of living have been cruel to them. They become disoriented and lost. They wander aimlessly, attempting to restore the relative tranquility of their former lives. Their sense of direction is dampened by the experience of trauma and many do not know how or where to begin to recover. They find themselves leaderless and alone. Their self-confidence is shattered and their courage is diminished. Some have even voiced their thoughts saying, "If only I had a map to get me out of this mess. If I knew where to start and where to go and how to get there, it would all be so much easier. If someone could tell what I might face and how long this journey of recovery would take and the things I should do to work my way out of my confusion, I think I could survive. But I am doubtful because I do not know what I am facing. I need roadmap."

For many, this book will serve as a roadmap. It will help guide and direct and it will point out some highs and lows of the recovery journey. It will help them to understand that the only clock that is important in their recovery is their own. It will present encouragement from those who have taken a similar journey; those who have, in fact, developed the recovery roadmap this book represents. They wish you Best Wishes on your own journey.

Chapter 1

Explosion
December 3, 1956

I have often been asked what sparked my interest in disaster, Crisis Intervention and Critical Incident Stress Management. I have joked (only partially) in response that I began my work when I was eight years old. The fact is, however, I was really only eight when it started for me. I will describe the events of December 3, 1956 in some detail since it was the event that generated my interest in disaster work and crisis intervention.

I went to school at St. Michael's Catholic School in Brooklyn, New York. It was located at 42nd street and 4th Ave. My family had an apartment on 40th street close to 5th avenue. Three blocks to walk to school and three blocks back home again. Not bad, it was about ¼ of a mile. At that time, it was just how you got to school in Brooklyn.

December 3, 1956 was a Monday. It was generally cloudy with a little rain here and there. Occasionally the sun peeked through the clouds. There was a fairly steady wind of about 10 miles per hour and the temperature was in the mid 40s. It was a typical school day in late fall.

School ended at 3:00 p.m. I helped one of my friends clean the black boards, clapped the erasers outside, (never on the bricks, only clapped together - the nuns had strict rules). I then picked up my book bag, said goodbye to my teacher and my buddy, and started for home. As I walked along I saw a cloud of smoke rise from Bush Terminal. A few minutes later I heard fire engines and trucks heading to the scene. The cloud turned very black and grew bigger and bigger as I went along. The closer I got, the higher the cloud rose, reaching way into the sky. I thought of my uncle Ed, who was on a ladder truck from 5th avenue about ten blocks from our apartment. I thought he might be on this fire. I would ask him about the fire the next time I saw him. He was always good for a story.

Bush Terminal was a huge facility. During World War II, it shipped war materials and equipment to Europe to supply our soldiers. It had docks, rail lines, ships, warehouses, sheds, roads, and lots of trucks, forklifts, cranes, and equipment that I never could understand or identify. About 25,000 people worked there. My parents would not allow any of my brothers or sisters or me to go anywhere near Bush Terminal. They thought it was just too dangerous and there were rough people there, who, I was told, should not be trusted.

When I reached 41st and 4th avenue, three boys I knew came down the hill on 41st. They were in the other classes at my school. I knew them, but not all that well. They saw me and stopped. They said they were going to the fire and I should go with them. This was one of those crucial moments. I hesitated and thought of my mother's reaction if she found out that I went near Bush Terminal. I decided her wrath was not worth the excitement of watching the fire. I said "no" and then endured a round of name-calling – "baby," "momma's boy," "sissy," and "fairy," before they rode off toward the growing fire.

My brother, Don, met me at the door. "Let's go look out the window in the front room and see the fire," he said. I could always count on him to get me involved in some adventure or another. He told me that one of our brothers, Doug, was eating a snack in the kitchen. The only other person in the apartment was our mother. He said we would have to be quiet because Mom was sleeping. She worked nights in a bank, processing the receipts for the day. She usually came home, cleaned the apartment, did the laundry, and went shopping before she slept. Then she would get up and get dinner ready for all of us. After dinner she made sure our homework was done before we were allowed to watch our black and white television. She and my Dad shared a foldout bed in the living room and Don and I had to quietly pass through her room to get to the front room. We gently closed the French doors between the rooms, so as not to wake my mother and we carefully opened the window and had a clear view of the fire and smoke. We actually saw the flames shooting up a hundred to two hundred feet into the sky. The clouds of thick black smoke filled the sky. The fire was only five blocks away; it was big. We heard some pops and crackling noises from the fire. There were sirens coming from every direction. More and more sirens were blaring and the bells clanging as they approached the area. We heard a ship's horn blowing continuously.

In about ten minutes there was a mushroom type cloud and large pieces of material flew up in the air. All this occurred in an instant. In a fraction of a second we were hit with a blast wave and the loudest sound I have ever heard in my life. Words cannot be found to describe the intensity of the explosion. The blast wave bowled Don and me across the floor as the French doors swung open with a jolt. My mother jumped up from her bed and screamed at my brother and me, "What did you do?" "What did you do?" Then she could see that Don and I were entangled together by our limbs and probably looked dazed to her. She ran toward the kitchen and we could hear her yelling at Doug, "What did you do?" He was covered with all the pots and pans that had been knocked off the shelves by the force of the explosion shaking the building. We never found the chocolate donut that Don was eating when we were looking out the window. . A mystery.

My mother spoke rapidly with a thick Irish accent. Up to this point I had only heard her speak perfect Brooklyn. Suddenly we had this Irish woman rapid firing questions through a thick Irish brogue. She asked questions, but did not wait for an answer. "Did the apartment building explode?" "Is it the boiler?" "Is it going to happen again?" "What broke?" "Who opened that window?" "It is cold in here." "I know something broke, I heard a lot of glass breaking?" "Did you break something?" "Do we need to get out?" "Is the building on fire?" "Where is your sister?" "What happened?"....

We checked the apartment. Nothing burning. Nothing broke. A few things knocked over. Lots of pots and pans lay scattered across the kitchen floor. Perhaps having a few partially opened windows spared us the loss of our windows. Neighbors all around us lost their windows. Neighbors called out to others to see if they were okay. People ran out of their apartments asking others if they were okay. More sirens seemed to come from all directions. People in the apartment building came to each other's doors. People spoke loudly. Rumors started to fly. Some said many firefighters were probably killed in the massive explosion. I thought of my uncle Ed. We all felt relief when all of my brothers and sisters got home. We worried about Ed. We waited for Dad to get home from work. Life was definitely unsettled. The fire was under control within a few hours but continued to burn through the night and into the next day. Uncle Ed called in the morning. Relief.

In answer to my mother's last question, "What happened?" here is what is known about the disaster. The fire originated on a pier operated by the Luckenbach Steamship Co., Inc. The fire on the 35th street pier began at 3:15 p.m. when sparks from a welding torch hit 26,365 pounds of flammable ground-up rubber foam. The fire grew rapidly with great heat and the thickest, blackest smoke imaginable. The Fire Department of New York was notified one minute later. The first engines and a nearby fireboat were on scene within a few moments and immediately called for a 2nd alarm assignment. The 3rd, 4th, and 5th alarms were called in approximately every 7 minutes after the second alarm. The arrivals of the 4th and 5th alarm units were delayed by heavy traffic and that may have contributed to the saving of firefighter lives. The blast occurred at 3:41 p.m. when the fire came in contact with 37,000 pounds of a class C explosive known as Cordeau Detonant Fuse (Prima Cord) which was illegally stored on the dock. It was designed to trigger TNT explosions.

The blast was equivalent to the simultaneous detonation of four 500-pound bombs. It was the largest explosion in New York City's history. A piece of hot steel landed a half-mile away and started a secondary fire. Spot fires from flaming debris popped up in all directions. Ten people died and 270 people were injured. A number of firefighters were blown into the water. The fireboat, *Firefighter,* was damaged in the explosion and one of its engines stopped operating. Had the fireboat not been ordered to move two hundred feet closer to shore than it was in its original position, the fireboat would have been within feet of the blast and it is unlikely that the fireboat or the crew would have survived. Several firefighters were injured but thankfully *none* were killed. This incident was nicknamed the "miracle on 35th street" by fire service personnel. Windows were broken for a mile in every direction. The explosion was heard 35 miles away. Property damage was over $10,000,000.

Among the dead were the boys who had asked me to go to the fire.

From that day forward, I was fascinated with disasters and read all about them. In time, I established a sufficient foundation of knowledge about disasters that it became a focal point for my interest in Crisis Intervention. It certainly contributed to my desire to serve as a paramedic and a volunteer firefighter. Eventually, my special interests in disaster and crisis intervention lead me to develop the Critical Incident Stress Management system to support emergency personnel, hospital employees, the military, and other organizations and businesses exposed to traumatic events. It all started when I was eight years old!

- JTM -

Crisis Concepts and Precepts

Lesson 1
"A Personal Crisis Lesson
December 3, 1956"

I remained distressed about the explosion for a long time. I did not know what that meant at first. At first it was because I worried about my Uncle Ed. The more I saw him, the less anxious I was about him. He was not involved at the Bush Terminal explosion and was just fine. *Facts reduced my anxiety.*

The real cause of my distress slowly crept into my consciousness. Twice, in a short period of time, I was exposed to the loss of life. First, my grandmother had died during the year and I attended the first funeral of my life. I was very attached to her and her loss was very painful for me. It took some time to stop thinking about her constantly. The sadness gradually lifted. It took time for my eight-year-old brain to deal with her loss, but it eventually happened and I moved on to other things that attracted my attention. I do not think I worked at dealing with her loss. It just happened over time. Gradually I could not remember what she sounded like. After a long time I could only remember how she looked when I saw a picture of her.

Second, the boys in my school who died in the explosion had an impact on me. It was not the same type of personal loss that I experienced with my grandmother's death. I did not know them that well and had no real personal attachment to them. It was less of a loss and more of a shock into reality. Had I gone with them, I could have been killed as well. It is very hard for an eight-year-old to grasp personal vulnerability and make sense out of it. In a crucial moment, my decision made a difference for my life.

- ❖ Traumatic stress reactions and grief can both last a long time.
- ❖ It is a big deal when an eight-year-old realizes he can die too.
- ❖ Accurate information is an anxiety antidote.

Chapter 2

Chances, Opportunities, Accidents, and Outcomes

On the outside chance that there might be shoes in the little Pennsylvania town of Gettysburg, two brigades of Confederate soldiers approached the town on the morning of July 1, 1863. They were under the command of Gen. Henry "Harry" Heth.

Heth had been a captain in US Army before the American Civil War. When hostilities broke out he was presented with the opportunity to switch sides and join the Confederate army. He chose to fight for his native state, Virginia. He worked for a while directly under Gen. Robert E. Lee as a quartermaster. That opportunity helped Heth's career. Lee made him a lieutenant colonel and later a brigadier general. Combat leadership soon followed.

Union cavalry patrols under the command of General John Buford happened to notice the dust clouds kicked up by the approaching foot soldiers. As dismounted cavalry, the Union patrols engaged the much larger force of Confederate soldiers by firing on them and then retreating. They repeated these actions until reinforcements arrived. The Confederates suffered considerable losses but they were successful in causing the Union forces to fall back to defensive positions on higher ground.

Both sides poured in reinforcements and the accidental engagement between the two relatively small military forces culminated in a monumental three-day battle involving nearly 100,000 combatants that generated a combined casualty count of nearly 50,000 soldiers. In the end, Gettysburg was a turning point in the war that the North was mostly losing until that battle.

There was a brief opportunity for the Union forces to pursue and destroy the Confederate forces before they could cross the Potomac River to relative safety in Virginia. For a number of reasons, Union leaders decided not to pursue the defeated Confederate forces. As a result, the war ground on for another 21 months with a great loss of life and the destruction of numerous towns and cities in the South.

In the American Civil War, the severe psychological reactions to the horrors of warfare were recognized and even named. Psychological reactions to war were categorized under the general name of "Soldier's Heart." Had there been medical personnel and military leaders who might have taken an interest in these reactions, early psychological intervention could have begun in the 1860's. The opportunities were present, but those crucial moments in time were missed and the opportunities dissipated.

A decade later, in the Franco-Prussian war in 1870-71, the French were desperate to return soldiers to the front lines. Paris was almost surrounded and the circumstances of the war looked bleak. Casualties were mounting and the French armies could not afford to have soldiers without obvious wounds taking up critical space in hospitals. Ordering them back to the front lines had no effect. Shooting those perceived to be deserters was an option, but living soldiers who might fight was a more desirable outcome. Medical personnel saw opportunities to take some chances and try some things that had never been tried before. They attempted to identify soldiers who seemed to be having the most psychological distress. They temporarily removed these soldiers from combat, but kept them within hearing distance of the cannon fire. They provided simple things like food, rest, fluids, and sometimes a medical person to talk to. The results were surprising and remarkable. Large numbers of soldiers seemed to recover with these simple procedures behind the front lines and they returned to combat. It was the first time that crisis intervention was provided in an organized and systematic manner.

– JTM –

Crisis Concepts and Precepts
Lesson 2
"A Brief History of Crisis Intervention"

The history of Crisis Intervention, begun under duress in the Franco Prussian War in 1870-71, continued, grew and expanded over the last century and a half, and continues to the present day. Crisis Intervention programs are serving many thousands of people around the globe every day.

Eduard Stierlin (1906) conducted one of the very first disaster studies involving Crisis Intervention when he applied crisis intervention procedures to the survivors and the family members of 1100 minors who were killed in the Courrieres mining disaster in northern France. Simple crisis intervention procedures learned in the Franco Prussian war were replicated in the Courrieres mining disaster with positive effect. In essence, Crisis Intervention consisted of providing basic care and respect for the victims of the tragedy.

In World War I, Dr. Thomas Salmon (1919) learned from the French what they were doing to assist their soldiers. He then systematically applied the same simple procedures with American soldiers and monitored the results. When distressed soldiers were temporarily removed from combat, but kept near the front lines, and then provided with rest, food, fluids, and emotional support, 65% returned to combat in 3-4 days. In contrast, if soldiers were removed from the front lines, brought to rear hospitals (transfer to the rear took about 24 hours), and then provided with the same support services only 40% returned to combat and that took 3-4 weeks.

The theories of Crisis Intervention were developed, discussed, researched, and put into action most especially through the work of Erik Lindermann and Gerald Caplan in the 1940s, 50s and 60s. The concepts and precepts of Crisis Intervention that they developed remain in use today. Lindermann and Caplan are credited with setting the foundation of Crisis Intervention. Developments and the addition of new advances in the field are established on the strong theoretical, historical, and practical foundations established by these two giants.

Their theories and practical applications were put to the test in the horrible and tragic Coconut Grove fire in Boston on November 28, 1942 in which 492 people lost their lives and 166 were injured. Lindermann used Crisis Intervention principles to support the survivors, their families, and the families of the deceased. Lindermann and his colleagues were also able to identify specific stages of grieving during the time he worked with those involved in the Coconut Grove fire.

By the 1950's Crisis Intervention was commonly applied in disaster work by the Red Cross and other disaster response organizations. Crisis Intervention services consisted of a broad spectrum of support services. It was very flexible and could be adjusted to the needs of the people involved in a particular disaster. Crisis Intervention as a group process was also being successfully applied to distressed families in the 1960s.

In the 1970s, Jeffrey T. Mitchell, one of the authors of this book began his work using Crisis Intervention with first response personnel – fire, law enforcement, and emergency medical personnel. Rapidly, the specific approaches to support distressed individuals and another set of procedures specifically developed to assist groups of first responders were being adopted by the military, government agencies, businesses, industries, organizations, school systems, and community groups. Crisis Intervention was organized into a comprehensive, integrated, systematic, and multi-tactic approach called Critical Incident Stress Management (CISM).

In 1989, the International Critical Incident Stress Foundation was developed to provide stress management and crisis intervention education, training, and support services to all of its constituent groups. The Foundation continues to provide services that have been accepted and endorsed by academic institutions and by numerous agencies and organizations including the United Nations. Today there are approximately 1,000 trained Critical Incident Stress Management teams serving around the world.

- ❖ **Critical Incidents** are powerful, traumatic events that initiate the crisis response.
- ❖ **Crisis** is a state of emotional turmoil. A crisis can also be defined as an acute emotional *reaction* to an intense stimulus.
- ❖ **Characteristics of a crisis:** 1) the usual balance between thinking and feeling is disrupted. 2) Usual coping mechanisms fail. 3) Distress, impairment, and dysfunction are present.
- ❖ **Two Types of crisis:** 1) *Maturational crises* occur as a result of changes in various stages of life, for

example, being a teenager, adulthood, mid-life, aging, or retirement. 2) *Situational crises* are caused by events like accidents, deaths, disaster, violence, property losses, illness, or threats

❖ **Psychological Trauma:** A traumatic experience is any event outside the usual realm of human experience and it is markedly distressing to those experiencing it. *Psychological Trauma* is the impact or damage done to a person after exposure to, among many things, combat, accidents, death of loved ones, life threatening illness, the experience of violence against one's person and destruction of cherished property. Such traumatic stressors usually involve the perceived threat to one's life or physical integrity or to the physical integrity of someone nearby us when we are spared from injury.

❖ **Traumatic Stress** is described as a broad range of cognitive, physical, emotional, spiritual, or behavioral *reactions* to a traumatic event. The term, *traumatic stress*, is loosely defined as a general, overall reaction in individuals or in groups after an exposure to a psychologically traumatizing event.

❖ **Crisis intervention** is a *temporary, active, and supportive* entry into a person's or a group's life experience during a period of intense emotional distress.

❖ **Goals of crisis intervention:** 1) reduce emotional tension 2) facilitate adaptive functions 3) identify people who need additional help and provide appropriate referrals.

❖ **Principles of Crisis Intervention:**
1. **Simplicity** – Interventions should be simple.

2. **Brevity** – It is typical to have 3-5 relatively short contacts to complete most crisis intervention work.

3. **Innovation** – Crisis Intervention should be creative and innovative. Novel solutions are often necessary.

4. **Pragmatism** – Suggestions must be practical if they are to work in resolving a crisis.

5. **Proximity** – Effective crisis intervention contacts occur closer to the operational zone or in someone's comfort zone.

6. **Immediacy** – A crisis reaction demands rapid intervention. Delays cause more pain and complications.

7. **Expectancy** – When possible, set up expectations of a reasonable positive outcome.

Note: At least six important crisis intervention principles were applied in the Franco-Prussian war. There was *innovation. Simple* support services were provided. The contacts were *brief* and *practical*. Finally support was provided close to the scene (*proximity*) and *immediately*. No mention is made in the literature as to whether or not positive outcome expectancy was discussed.

Chapter 3

Not Much

The question was inevitable. Every seven or eight year old boy in the 1950's, and many girls too, got around to it soon or later. "Daddy, what did you do during the war?" I remember being shocked and disappointed when his answer came after what seemed like an awfully long pause. "Not much." Stunned, I said, "What do you mean, Daddy." This was followed by another long pause. I pressed the point. "Daddy did you go to war. Did you fight somewhere?" His answer, "No, I didn't do much." I was bewildered. I wanted an answer and he was not offering anything to satisfy my curiosity.

I didn't know what to do. My classmates were all comparing stories about their Dads and what they did during the war. Some even had stories about their Moms and what they did to help build the ships that won the war. They were good stories and very exciting. They talked of their fathers as great heroes. They fought. They were in tanks, flew airplanes, fought the enemy from navy ships. They got medals. My Dad "...didn't do much." That was not something I wanted to tell my friends.

Over the years I tried several times to get him to answer my questions. He was a very private person and a humble person and he would not easily give up personal information about the war. One time he said that other men had done so much more than he. When I retorted with, "like what?" he pointed out men at the YMCA where he worked as the physical director. He would mention how this one had blown up a German machine gun position and saved his buddies. Another one had landed a plane safely even though he was badly wounded. Yet another had carried a fellow soldier off the battlefield while being shot at. When I redirected the question to him, I got the "not much" answer again.

While in college, I once had a two-week break in between work at a camp and the start of the school year. I spent as much time as possible with him. I asked him about the war again. He started off with his usual, "Well I didn't do much." This time, however, was different. He went on, "I taught men how to swim." A breakthrough! I said, "I know that you taught people how to swim because you were the Aquatics Director for the YMCA. What did that have to do with the war?"

"That's just it," he answered. "Every day they would bring truck loads of soldiers, sailors, marines and plane crews and I ran a program to teach them to swim." He went on to explain that in a week's time they knew how to tread water and they had at least three strokes they could use if they ended up in the water somewhere. They were taught freestyle, sidestroke, and breaststroke. "That is what I did in the war. So, not much."

I asked if he had been drafted and he said he had been drafted for service in the US Navy. He was required to go to a pre-induction interview at the Brooklyn Navy Yard. A navy officer asked him what he did for a living. He answered that he was an aquatics director for the YMCA.

Among the things he did was teaching people how to swim. The officer wanted to know how fast people could learn to swim. The answer was a few days to a week. Could a large group learn at the same time? Yes. The officer asked a few more questions about the process of learning to swim and then he excused himself and left the room. In a few minutes two or three navy officers were in the hallway looking at my father through the office window and carrying on a discussion. They went away and about an hour later the officer who was conducting the interview came in and told him that arrangements had been made with the YMCA where he worked to have him train military personnel to swim. The training was to be done in large groups. My father was not to join the navy. Instead, he was to spend the war doing what he did routinely, but now his work would be done on a grand scale and for the benefit of the military.

I asked him if he thought that his work might have saved some lives. He answered that it probably did. I suggested that he might be proud of that. He then told me that so many people he knew had died in the war. He felt ashamed that he went to his job everyday, taught young men how to swim and then went home at night to a meal and a warm bed. Meanwhile soldiers, sailors, pilots and the people he knew were fighting for their lives in the war and he felt he should have been there to help them.

In 1995, fifty years after the war ended, I was conducting a World Congress on Stress, Trauma, and Coping in Baltimore. Quentin Aanenson, a WWII fighter pilot was making a presentation. During my introduction of Mr. Aanenson, I related the story of my father's distress over not serving in a combat environment during the war and his inability to see that he made a valuable contribution. There were several WWII veterans in the audience who were there to listen to Mr. Aanenson. His presentation was powerful and the audience was enthralled. People flocked to the stage to shake his hand, make a comment, or ask a question. One elderly gentleman approached me directly and asked if he could have a word with me.

This veteran told me that he had learned to swim during the war in the program that my father ran for military personnel at the Prospect Park YMCA in Brooklyn, New York. He then said, "Tell your father that I went in at Normandy. I ended up in deep water when we had to go over the side of the boat because of the machine gun fire. What your father taught me saved my life. There are many who can say the same. I am alive today because of your father's training."

A week later I held my father's hand as I sat next to the bed in which he was gradually dying from Alzheimer's and Parkinson's. I waited for one of those crucial moments in which he had a bubble of clarity and I said, "A soldier named Jimmy told me to tell you that your learn-to-swim program during the war saved his life at Normandy. He said to tell you there are many like him. You did make a difference in the war." There was a slight smile and the bubble of clarity faded away.

–JTM –

Crisis Concepts and Precepts

Lesson 3
"A Crisis Remains a Crisis"

For most of my father's life, he believed that he did not do enough during WWII. He felt ashamed that he did not serve in a combat environment. He felt guilt that he was eating at home and sleeping in his own bed while others suffered on the battlefield far from the people they loved. He always felt that he should have done more to directly support the young men of his generation. He carried this personal trauma for his life because he never found a resolution. Maybe he felt some slight relief on his deathbed, but it is sad that he did not find a resolution earlier when he might have experienced life without the guilt and shame he felt because he did his job and helped our nation through some of its darkest hours. The affirmation that he had saved lives did not arrive early enough. He died carrying most of the burden he had taken on over fifty years earlier.

❖ A crisis remains a crisis until some resolution is found. It doesn't matter if it is 5 minutes or 50 years, or a lifetime. People may suppress their crisis reactions and continue on with life, but they will always be seeking a resolution to the distress caused by some event or circumstance they survived. This is so even if they do not realize it. It is so even if they never ask for assistance.

❖ It is never too late to help somebody find a partial or complete resolution of his or her pain. When we recognize their pain, there may be opportunities at work; the chance to relieve pain and make a difference for them may be present for just a few crucial moments. A small effort on our part may make a huge difference for another human being.

❖ Trying something is better than doing nothing. If something might help someone, we should give it a try. Maybe we will fail. Maybe we won't. We will not know unless we try.

❖ Crisis reactions often have more to do with perceptions than facts. My father did what his country needed at the time. He followed orders. He believed, however, that he had abandoned his friends. He felt ashamed. He could not see the reality of the situation. He had, in fact, contributed to the saving of hundreds, if not thousands, of soldiers, sailors, and airmen in WWII.

❖ Gerald Caplan, MD once said at a conference on crisis and stress, "Excellent help may be given by family members, friends, and colleagues who lack formal psychological education" (1972 – Baltimore, Maryland).

❖ Helping someone may only take one crucial moment. All you have to do is decide to reach out and try to make a difference.

Chapter 4

The Decision

The world was a rough place to live in 1956.

- Egypt was threatening to invade Palestine.
- A primitive tribe in Ecuador murdered five US missionaries.
- Soviet armed forces crushed demonstrations in the republic of Georgia.
- Ninety-six US congressmen signed a protest against the 1954 Supreme Court ruling that desegregated public schools.
- TWA and United airliners collided over the Grand Canyon killing 128 people.
- The SS *Andrea Doria* and the SS *Stockholm* collided in fog. The Andrea Doria sank and 51 people were killed.
- Britain, France and Israel began military operations to invade Egypt and open the Suez Canal. Intense combat followed.
- Hungary revolted against the Soviet Union. Soviet forces invaded Hungary and brutally crushed the revolt. Thousands of Hungarians were killed and a quarter of a million Hungarians left the country.
- Nikita Khrushchev threatened the US - "We will bury you!"

- Fidel Castro invaded Cuba and began his revolt.

  New York's "Mad Bomber" planted a bomb in the Paramount Movie Theatre in Brooklyn

- Brooklyn Marine Terminal disaster.
- My grandmother died and I was only eight years old.

On the evening of December 2, 1956 a crude homemade bomb exploded in the crowded Paramount Movie Theatre in Brooklyn, New York. There were approximately 1500 people in the theatre at the time. Six people were injured. New York's "Mad Bomber" had struck again. He had been terrorizing the city for fifteen years.

New Yorkers were emotionally shaken up. Newspapers reported the city to be "paralyzed" and "gripped by fear." New Yorkers were living through a reign of terror. The fifteen-year police hunt had failed to uncover the suspect's identity or whereabouts.

Over the fifteen years of terror, about 35 bombs had been placed in train stations, on trains, in phone booths, in theatres, at Radio City Music Hall, in Grand Central Station, in libraries, and other public places in Manhattan and Brooklyn. Twenty-two of the bombs exploded and a total of 15 people were injured. Any pubic places, including schools, were vulnerable. Parents were terrified to send their children to school and some opted to keep their children home on the morning of December 3, 1956, the day after the blast at the Paramount Theatre in Brooklyn.

Loren and Rita Mitchell read the morning newspapers reporting on the most recent bombing the evening before. They discussed the safety of their six children and whether or not it would be wise to keep them home from school for the day.

Rita was an immigrant from Wexford, Ireland and she had lived through the troubled years leading up to the 1919 Irish revolt. She knew of bombings in her native Ireland. She knew that people rumored to be agents of the English government had murdered her grandfather, who was active in the Irish republican politics. She knew how fear could disrupt one's life. That event triggered her mother and father's decision to move the family from Ireland to the United States. It also helped Rita to build up her resilience to turmoil and threat.

Loren came from Hudson Falls, New York near Lake George. He was a descendent of one of the Green Mountain Boys who had taken Fort Ticonderoga, the great stone fort between Lake George and Lake Champlain in northeastern New York State during the American Revolution. The fort fell without a shot being fired after the invaders captured the fort's commander. Ticonderoga's cannons were taken by the patriots and thundered against the British in several Revolutionary War engagements.

Loren and Rita agreed that no one would progress in life without a good education. They both agreed that their children could not get that education if they stayed home from school too often. Illness might be a legitimate, but rarely utilized, excuse in the Mitchell household. Non-specific anxiety and fear was not an acceptable reason for missing school. They also agreed that fear could paralyze people and everyone had to remain in control of their emotions in order to make rational decisions. Fear had not stopped their ancestors from doing what was right. Fear would not deprive their children of an education. It was time to get the kids up for school.

Epilog: The December 2, 1956 bombing was the last bomb planted by the Mad Bomber. Police tried a different tactic. They attempted to communicate with the perpetrator via an open letter in the newspapers. They carefully reviewed the hundreds of letters they received in response. Information provided by Con Edison employees gave some clues that, when combined with statements in one of the responses, helped to crack the case. Within a month, police arrested a disgruntled and mentally unstable former employee of the Con Edison Company who had been injured in a 1940 accident. He felt that he had not been treated fairly and received no compensation for his permanent injuries. He planted bombs to get people to pay attention to how unfair he felt Con Edison treated him. In his distorted thinking, he assumed that the company would make things right if he bombed enough.

– JTM –

Crisis Concepts and Precepts

Lesson 4
"Critical Incident Stress Management"

There was no organized approach to assisting New York's citizens through the emotional turmoil created by the Mad Bomber. The primary forms of communication were the newspapers and the radio. Rumors abounded. No one had yet organized crisis management services that could assist people with decision-making and guidelines to help their families. Experts in traumatic stress were rare at the time and there were, in fact, few psychiatrists, psychologists, social workers or counselors providing general mental health services in the communities. Unless someone was experiencing severe mental disturbance, few people came onto contact with mental health professionals. Psychiatric services were also perceived to be a luxury for the rich. Few average citizens in the 1950's could afford to engage in such services. Much of the history of Crisis Intervention and Critical Incident Stress Management was still to be written. It was an eight year old child's experience of fear and confusion that eventually led to the development of Critical Incident Stress Management services that would fill the informational gap and provide free guidance, facts, and support in times of crisis to emergency services personnel and to the general population.

Years later the child's fear and distress was channeled into the development of the Critical Incident Stress

Management (CISM) program as an organized approach to Crisis Intervention. It contains a package of Crisis Intervention techniques. CISM is a subdivision of the main field of Crisis Intervention. Crisis Intervention is the larger, 'parent' field, and CISM is an offshoot or a subset of that field. As a subset it shares in the history, theory base, research, practices and procedures of the parent field.

A subset has some differences from the main field. Crisis Intervention covers many more situations than does CISM. For example, child abuse, elder abuse, marital or relationship dysfunction, uncontrolled rage, anti-social behaviors, significant behavioral problems, alcohol problems and substance abuse are certainly covered in the general field of Crisis Intervention. In CISM, these issues are recognized and steps to save lives and assure safety and security are immediately provided, but these situations are matters for referral to professional mental health personnel. CISM's role is to assist until a referral resource can take over the intervention. The primary focus of CISM is to support people who are exposed to work related traumatic events. Trained CISM personnel should have sufficient training to handle most crises whether they are directly related to work or more associated with personal issues. There are areas, such as those mentioned above, that they will refer as quickly as possible.

Mental health professionals may provide Crisis Intervention services as a means to assess a client and get the person prepared for psychotherapy. Crisis Intervention and its subset, Critical Incident Stress Management, are not considered psychotherapy nor are they a substitute for psychotherapy. They are support services. This is especially so when they are provided by people who lack formal psychological or psychiatric education.

The most frequent providers of Critical Incident Stress Management (CISM) support services are, in no particular order, nurses, emergency medical technicians and paramedics, police officers, firefighters, search and rescue personnel, military personnel, clergy and chaplains. We can easily add to this list, parents, teachers, coaches, friends, family members, and colleagues.

The initials, **CISM**, can be applied in two ways.

First, the initials are the <u>title</u> of the Crisis Intervention program: *CISM*
C – Critical
I – Incident
S – Stress
M – Management

Second, the initials stand for a <u>description</u> of a specific Crisis Intervention program:

C - *Comprehensive*
I - *Integrated*
S - *Systematic*
M - *Multicomponent*

Comprehensive means that the program has elements in place <u>before</u> a crisis appears. A CISM program also has essential services available <u>during</u> and <u>after</u> a crisis

Integrated means that the program blends and combines techniques and interventions so that no one element stands alone. The research strongly suggests that combinations of interventions are more effective than stand alone interventions.

Systematic means that the interventions in this Crisis Intervention program are applied in a logical sequential order. For example, assessment and planning is completed before initiating individual or group interventions.

Multicomponent means that the CISM program has many parts ranging from individual support to assistance to families, groups and organizations.

Tools of Critical Incident Stress Management

CISM services are best delivered by means of an organized and systematic program. Certain features should be in place before a critical incident strikes. For example, pre-crisis education, policy and protocol development, resistance training, and strategic planning can be instituted to prepare to manage a critical incident and the resulting critical incident stress reactions.

There are a number of CISM tools that may be applied as the event unfolds. Assessment, incident-specific strategic planning, informational group interventions, individual crisis intervention and advice to management are typical during an event.

After a critical incident, CISM techniques include, but are not limited to, interactive group interventions, individual support, significant other support services, follow-up services and post-incident education. All the parts of a CISM program should be interrelated and linked. They are applied systematically which means there is a logical order to the use of interventions.

The most common crisis intervention tools in a CISM program are:

- Pre-incident planning, policy development, training, education,

- Crisis assessment

- Strategic planning

- Individual crisis intervention

- Informational group interventions (Rest Information and transition Services, Crisis Management Briefing). Had it existed at the time, the Crisis Management Briefing (CMB) would have been an excellent tool to provide information and guidance to the citizens of New York who were suffering in fear over the actions of the Mad Bomber. The CMB is a meeting in which community leaders provide facts and information to manage the situation and trained crisis intervention specialists provide stress management information and guidelines that can help individuals, families and community members deal with their distress.

- Interactive group crisis interventions (Defusing, Critical Incident Stress Debriefing {CISD})

- Pastoral crisis intervention

- Family support services

- Significant other support services

- Follow-up services

- Referral services

- Follow-up meetings with communities impacted by a critical incident to determine additional needs

- Post-incident education

- Links to pre-incident planning and preparation for the next critical incident

Chapter 5

A Closet Full of Courage

As my father pulled the covers up to my chin, he promised me that there were no monsters in the closet. I asked my father if he would also place my favorite blanket on top of me and he did. As his words, "sleep tight," faded into the dark room, the door closed behind him. The room was so dark and I knew that there were monsters in the closet. Even though my blanket, to me, was an iron blanket and would protect me from the dark closet, it wasn't enough to make me sleep tight. I ran to the closet door and turned on the light switch. I ran back to my bed and crawled under my covers and made sure my iron blanket was on top of me. My older brother who had remained quiet through this whole ordeal told me to turn the light off but soon we were both asleep.

In the morning I woke to the smell of waffles. As I walked into the kitchen dragging my blanket behind me, my father was just finishing his waffles. He told me how proud he was of me and that I had shown great courage to sleep with the closet light off. My brother just sat there at the kitchen table and, for once, he did not give me up. My father was rolling his red handkerchief up and tying it around his head to be used as a sweatband. My mother was filling up his Mason jar full of water and ice. As my father went out the door to do his Saturday jobs around the house, he told me how proud he was of me. I think that was the first time that anyone had told me that I was a courageous boy. I knew that I was not really courageous but I wanted my father to be proud of me.

For several years after that, I went everywhere with my iron blanket. The only time that my mother could wash the iron blanket was when I was already asleep. I traded my iron blanket for a Mickey Mouse swimming suit. In my mind the suit gave me special powers. The suit made it possible for me to stay afloat when swimming. The suit also made it possible for me to climb trees. Once while at church, I was sitting on the church pew and my mother noticed that I was squirming around. She told me to lean forward and she pulled back my pants and discovered that instead of underwear I was wearing my Mickey Mouse swimming suit. That was not the first time that I had worn my suit for underwear. Sometimes I would wear my underwear on top of my swimming suit but she soon figured that trick out.

As I grew older, I always had something that would bring me good luck or protect me from things that I did not know about. Sometimes the things that I did not know about were the bigger boys that sat at the back of the school bus, or a woman who asked me to try some white powder that would make me feel good. No matter what the situation, I would tell my parents and they would tell me that I was very courageous. I soon learned that courage meant that I had the ability to conquer and survive any situation. I would read stories in the history books at school and they would talk about courageous soldiers and how they died fighting in battle. To me I had become a courageous person.

* * *

As we pulled up to the house the sound of me fastening my Velcro echoed through my ears. I wanted to make sure that my bulletproof vest was tight against my body. As we moved across the yard with our weapons drawn, I could feel my good luck items pressing against my thighs. In my watch pocket was a silver dollar given to me by my father. In my front pants pocket was a small birdcall given to me by my wife. Next to it was a small flat stone also given to me by my wife. She found it when we walked on the beach during our honeymoon. In the other pants pocket was a prayer card that has the prayer of St. Joseph on it. My father gave it to me nine years before and all that was left of it is a small piece of plastic and some unreadable words. Around my neck is the medal of St. Michael the Archangel. He is the saint for police officers. My wife gave me that.

We knocked on the door and yelled, "police with a search warrant." The door was opened. We moved through the house like a centipede and made sure there were no monsters in the closets. Once we were sure the house was safe, we put our weapons back in their holsters. Yes, the courageous little boy had become a police officer and this was my first federal search warrant. I had been in law enforcement for nine years but I was just hired by the agency where I always wanted to work. This was my case and I wanted to make sure that I did not make any mistakes. As my boss walked out of the house, she had a look on her face as if she were a million miles away. I asked her if everything was all right and she said yes. As she walked to her car, she mumbled, "That place looks familiar."

In my nine years of policing, I too had seen several places like this. A doublewide mobile home with several additions added on to it. There was a car on blocks in the front yard. An old dog was chained up to a tree with his manure surrounding him. His tail did not wag but instead found a safer home between his legs. The inside was not any better. A faucet dripped in the kitchen and piles of dirty dishes waited to be cleaned. Roaches ran into the dark comers as we walked across the kitchen floor. Mounds of dirty clothes filled every corner of every room. The cat's litter box had not been cleaned in several weeks and the smell of manure reeked through the house. We found what we were looking for and we called it a day. As we drove away from the house, I could not ignore the look on my boss's face.

Several weeks passed and I wanted to know what caused that look on her face. One day, after a meeting, we decided to stop at a restaurant and have some late breakfast. I had waffles and she had eggs and sausage. I asked her why she had that look on the day we served the search warrant. She said it was a long story. I asked if I had done something wrong that day and she said "no."

I took a big bite of a waffle and she told me her story. She said she was raised on a poor dirt farm in the south. She referred to herself as coming from "white trash." The house where we served the search warrant reminded her of the house she was raised in. She said her father was a blue-collar worker and her mother was just that, a mother. What made her house even more 'special' was the way her father would show his affection. Instead of pulling the covers up to the children's chins at bedtime, he would beat the children. She said he never sexually molested them but he would beat them and verbally abuse them. She said that during her whole childhood she was told she was nothing more than trash on the side of the road.

She knew the only way she could escape her monster was to become very good at sports. She received a scholarship from a college and finally escaped. She thought that she would be safe from the monster but he was so deep inside her that the battle had just begun. She had a closet full of low self-esteem and dark corners that were now too small to hide in. She could only find peace in the bottom of a liquor bottle. When she was so drunk that the monster would finally go away, she would find herself searching for her mother and that rocking chair. When her mother and the rocking chair could not be found, she would curl up in the corner and stroke her own hair until she fell asleep. She said this went on for years and she soon learned that she needed to seek counseling. Counseling helped her deal with the monster and she decided to become a social worker so she could show the other pieces of trash that they can escape the monsters. Since she was very physically fit, she decided to become a fire fighter. After several years as a fire fighter she went to work for a federal law enforcement agency.

I had just finished my last waffle and her words made it difficult for me to swallow. It was difficult for me to imagine that the worst monster that she had encountered in her lifetime was not hiding in a closet but she called him Dad. I asked if her father was still alive and she said no. She said in the last ten years of his life he became lost inside his own mind. The doctors called it Alzheimer's but she believes the dark corners of the closet that he searched for the children to beat had gotten the best of him. Her mother took care of him in his final years and on some rare occasions he would tell my boss how proud he was of her. She said those words felt good but she was never sure if that was the monster talking or God trying to help him repair the damage he had done to her.

For years she had held some anger toward her mother but she forgave her and held tight to the comforting sound of the rocking chair being rocked and most of all she can still feel the soft strokes in her hair from her mother hands.

As her story came to an end I just sat there and looked at our empty plates and that was how I felt, empty. I searched for the words that may help soothe the wounds left by her father but all I could do was swallow. We both were in the same profession but we were originally attracted to the job for much different reasons. From a small child I was convinced I was a very courageous person. I always knew I would grow up and become a solider, fire fighter, or police officer. These jobs require me to be courageous. My boss became a fire fighter because she wanted to help people and she went into federal law enforcement to help people in a different way. I became a police officer because I was a courageous person. After my first year I realized it felt real good to help people who sometimes cannot help themselves. I looked up and saw the most courageous person I had ever met.

I have lots of friends who are veterans of war. I have friends who have been shot in the line of duty. But none of them had to fight for their life the second they took their first baby breaths. All of her childhood years were a battle to stay alive and she still fights today. For the first time in my life the word courage had a whole new meaning. I thought courage meant to conquer and defeat your enemy. Courage, to my boss meant escaping and dealing with a monster that was ingrained into her soul, mind, body and most of all her spirit. Every day she recalls the 18 years she was told that she was nothing more than trash on the side of the road. When she remembers his abusive words and recalls his strong hands hitting her, she wants to crawl under the bed to escape but instead she puts on her running shoes. She runs down the road and past the cornfield that reminds her of one of her childhood hiding places. As one foot follows the other the sound of her shoes landing on the pavement sounds like the rolling of the rocking chair and she finds peace at the end of a ten-mile run.

As for her mother, she still lives on the same dirt farm and spends her days being independent. As for my boss, she too lives on a farm and spends her weekends being independent. She has an assortment of animals there. Most of them were trash that no one else wanted. A cat with no rear legs and several dogs that just wanted to be petted not kicked. The dogs wag their tails and are never chained to a tree. The litter box is cleaned everyday and a stray cat now knows where to find a meal. She has a few horses and they have made her a grandma more than once.

A few weeks after she told me her story I walked into her office. I reached into my pocket and pulled out what is left of my St. Joseph prayer card. I told her the story behind the card and how long I have carried it. I handed her a brand new St. Joseph card from my other hand. I told her that I could not guarantee that the card would protect her from the monster she called Dad. But I did believe it would protect her from monsters that the rest of us have to deal with. She reached out and took the card and smiled. In a job some police officers call thankless, today was not one of those days. Today I helped someone who had more courage than me and she wasn't a veteran but a small beaten little child who just wanted to grow up and be a woman.

I do not understand why people like her father are put on this earth. There are a lot of things that I do not understand. I have learned to live with them, but I will never just accept them. As for me, I thank God my father told me I was courageous and my brother did not give me up. I am glad my mother let me wear my Mickey Mouse swimming suit for underwear sometimes. Most of all, I thank my personal saint, my wife. She doesn't laugh at a full-grown man who carries two coins, a flat rock, a birdcall, and a nine-year-old prayer card in his pocket everyday.

Written by a courageous little boy.

- WLV -

Crisis Concepts and Precepts

Lesson 5
"Resistance, Resilience, Recovery"

The underpinning for Critical Incident Stress Management is **Resiliency.** To be most effective, CISM relies on a certain amount of built-in toughness or hardiness in the human spirit. Even when people are at their lowest point and they feel broken and hopeless, CISM attempts to help them to reach down deep inside themselves and find the remaining natural strength or pliability that holds them together during tumultuous times.

We are each born with a certain amount of elasticity that allows us to bend without breaking. One expert on human resiliency, Dr. Glen Schiraldi, tells us that resilience is "standard issue." We are issued resilience at birth. It can be stretched and beaten out of shape and under extraordinary circumstance it might even be broken. Typically, however, resiliency gives us the power to pick ourselves up and continue with our lives even when the odds are against us.

The story in Chapter 5 is an excellent example of a young girl who was emotionally and physically abused by her father for the first 18 years of her life. Yet she became an athlete and used that achievement as a means to pull herself out of the quagmire represented by her home life. She made herself into a successful law enforcement command officer. She made a contribution to life despite the horrible conditions of her early development. That's resilience.

There are three components of resiliency. They are resistance, resilience, and recovery.

Resistance is the ability of individuals, groups, organizations and entire populations to resist distress, impairment and dysfunction. Resistance can be developed and enhanced. Training, education, healthy living and enriched life style behaviors, and attitudes long before the traumatic event strikes are the best methods to develop resistance. In a loose sense of the word resistance equates, in a way, to a certain degree of immunity. The more we can build resistance in our lives, the better able we will be to protect ourselves from the harm caused by traumatic events and other stressful pressures. If we build resistance we also enhance resilience. Resistance is development of protective factors to make us stress-resistant. Protective factors include self-esteem, optimism, improved nutrition, appropriate sleep habits, social support, family life, exercise, and avoidance of non-prescription drugs and tobacco, and limitation of alcohol use.

Resilience is the ability to bounce back from adversity. It is the human capacity to bend under the strain of pressure and pain, but to get back up or rebound and continue on and work against difficulties and remain successful and engaged in life.

Recovery is the resolution, repair, reconstruction, restoration, and rebuilding of the human spirit, mind, and body after sustaining the damages incurred by prolonged, extreme, or overwhelming distress. Recovery implies that the person sustained considerable psychological and sometimes physical damage. Psychotherapy and medical treatment is frequently indicated in such cases. People need rest, a reduction in pressure and stress, time to work things through, companionship, reassurance, and direct support. Most often they need to find a personal meaning in their experience of the tragedy before they can resume their life. It takes a lot of healing to work one's way through the recovery process.

NOTE: Sometimes we will be lost for words when we listen to the painful story of another. The exact things to say are not that important. What is of the greatest importance is that we took the time to listen and that we were totally engaged in listening. What people need most is not our words or our advice, but to be listened to and heard. Sometimes when we listen really carefully, they can hear themselves and find their own way out of the darkness.

Chapter 6

Tears from Heaven

I heard my mom in the kitchen below my room and I already felt the hot summer air coming through my bedroom window. I decided to get up and head down for breakfast. My mom had breakfast ready for me and told me that dad wanted me to go out to the field and straighten up the corn that was blown over from the hard rain we had last night. I walked between the cornrows and felt the earth find a place between my toes. I brushed up against the corn stalks and they were still wet from last night. I walked back to the house and attempted to wash the earth from my toes but it just seemed to linger there.

As I drove down the gravel road I thought of that day as we passed the corn growing on both sides of the car. The corn was about the same height but I was taller and much older. I met the woman next to me the day before in an airport. She was sent to this place like me to try and help a group of men recover from a day no one could imagine. I named her in my head within in minutes of meeting her, "the city girl." She was complex in some respects but had a sense of pure genuineness despite her lack of knowledge of life beyond the sidewalks. At the end of the gravel road was a modest farmhouse in the middle of that cornfield; it reminded me of the farms I worked on as I grew up. A woman old enough to be my mother greeted us at the door and she had a smile on her face. We walked into the living room and in a wheel chair was a man I had flown half a day to see. He immediately reminded me of my father by his face and the fact that my father spent the last years of his life in a wheel chair. I shook his hand that was worn like his face. I explained to him that I was sent here to talk to him about the event that killed many but which he survived. He said in his soft voice "Not much to talk about." I said, "Ok, but will you listen to me?" He said, "Yes." I talked about how important it is to talk about the event and how it's not good to keep it buried inside you but he just sat there playing with his hands.

I reached in my pocket and pulled out a United States Marine Corps key chain. I told him when I found out I was coming to this spot on the map I went to my shooting range and taped this key chain up at 100 yards. I found that sweet spot on my rifle stock, controlled my breathing, and focused on the task at hand. I placed one round through the center of the key chain. I told him on days when the wind behaves and I have my head screwed on straight I can do it out to 300 yards but not on the day before I came here. He took the key chain and said, "I was a Marine in Vietnam." I could see a small tear squeeze from his eye as I too could feel one squeeze from mine. I told him on the other side of the key chain was St. Michael and he said, "I'm also a Catholic." By now that tear I felt was rolling down my check and there was one rolling down his. His wife who had been sitting by his side the whole time we talked was also in tears. I turned to the city girl who had sat there not saying a word and she too was in tears. I named him in my head "the old devil dog." A name used to describe the toughest Marines. He survived Vietnam and came home to survive an event that killed many and temporally left him in a wheel chair.

As the city girl and I drove away from the house I stared down the cornrows and wished I were there. I wished at the end of those cornrows my dad would be standing there and tell me it was going to be ok. The city girl said "Are you ok?" I said, "I'm fine, that one just hit close to home."

My father had one job working in the rock quarry but many more jobs on our small farm. My father was also a beekeeper. This small town reminded me of a beehive that decides to swarm. When the queen bee leaves the hive the worker bees follow; it's a very confusing time for the hive until the queen lands and the worker bees surround her. As we drove though the town there were cars everywhere and news crews on every corner. The city girl and I went to the local fire station to see if we could find some workers that were confused from the event that had taken some of their own. I saw a middle aged woman in the station who I immediately named the "mother hen." You could tell she had a handle on it all and was keeping it all under control. I walked up and told her who I was and why I was there, she said, not now. The inside of the station reminded me of the inside of a beehive. I could recall many times during a swarm my dad standing next to me and we would look down into the hive to see if the queen was still in there. The worker bees were frantically searching for her because they need a leader. There was an office in the station and we found a man younger than me sitting behind a desk. His dad was the old devil dog and he made it clear that as soon as his dad was able he would be back at his desk.

Over the next few days we were accepted into this place and our reason for coming here became a part of the recovery. I found myself talking to people in closets, on the tailgate of a truck, on the phone, in a car, any place we could find some privacy. I would visit the old devil dog everyday and he would always greet me with a smile. He never spoke of that day but he just talked about all the other days that were less painful. Our days were long and usually at the end of the day the city girl and I would have a meal where we could just talk about nothing. I would listen to her life and where she came from and I could not help but feel like we were two objects thrown in a tornado but clinging to each other trying to brace ourselves until the vortex of emotions stopped.

The mother hen finally came to see me as acceptable member to her flock and she started to send me her emotionally wounded members. She asked me to talk to this man who had been hiding out for a few days since the event. I immediately named him "the Dutchman." He somehow survived the event and was ready to talk about it. I listened to his story and reached in my pocket and removed a quarter that I had shot a hole through at 100 yards, he placed it on his key chain. I told him that it should remind him that no matter what, someone does care.

The old devil dog asked me to his house one day. He told me that he wanted me to talk to one of his guys that survived but was physically wounded. As the man walked in the house on crutches I immediately named him "the Fixer." The old devil dog explained to the fixer who I was and the fixer would not look at me. I talked to him for an hour and once in a while a tear would roll down his cheek but he seldom said a word. I reached in my pocket and handed him a United States Marine Corps key chain with a hole in it and explained what I do with them. He held the key chain in his hand and rubbed it like it was a magic lamp that would grant him a wish. A wish that day never happened. I asked him if there was anything he needed and he said I want to go back there. I said back where? "Where it happened," and I said, "ok."

The next day the city girl and I loaded the old devil dog and the fixer up and drove them back to that place. The city girl took the devil dog to his spot where he was standing when it happened and I took the fixer to his spot. The fixer navigated his crutches around the debris and never said a word until he stopped at a spot and said, "I was standing right here." He started to cry and so did I. For the first time since we met he looked up at me and said, "I have to go." I did my best to explain to him none of this was his fault and he did his best, but my words never made it to him. As I followed him through the debris I saw a small piece of our flag just laying there, an image that is burned in my mind. The fixer sat down in the car and I went over to close the door and he was still crying but started to tell me his story. It was a cloudy day and it did not look like it would rain but it started to sprinkle. I could not help but think it was tears from heaven.

He spoke of his friends who were in front of him and why did he survive and they died. This was my time to listen and I did. As it continued to rain and he continued to talk he said, "I want to see my truck." I explained his truck was very damaged and it was a long walk to his truck. He said I walked out of here and I can walk back in here. Once again we navigated our way through the debris and found what was left of his truck. He pointed to his tools strung all over the ground and said, "At least I got something to work with." He told me he would like to have his tools back. I said, "I will buy you some new tools" and he said, "no I want those tools; I want to remember that day." We walked back to the car and he talked more about that day.

The town was holding a memorial service for those who died on that day. The old devil dog asked me to go with him. As we rode to the memorial service I asked him who he talked to about things like that day. He said, "When I came back from Vietnam I put my head on my wife's shoulder and cried." I did not ask him that question again. There were a lot of people at the memorial service. I stood behind the old devil dog's wheel chair and looked across more caskets than I had ever seen in my life. I reached in my pocket and handed him a collection of Catholic medals and one quarter with a hole in it. I told him many years ago in the field behind my parent's home I taped a quarter to a fencepost at 50 yards. I laid my rifle down across a 55-gallon barrel and told my father to watch me punch a hole through that quarter. I got lucky and did. I made him a necklace with the quarter and as his health declined he added Catholic medals and wore it until the day he died. I told the old devil dog that this collection of medals helped my dad get though 13 years of hell and maybe on this day it will help him. He clutched the medals in one hand and in the other hand was his wife's hand. I don't recall much about the service but I do recall asking myself how I ended up here and why me. Why was I given this privilege to be here? Why was I given this honor to be with this man on this day?

The city girl and I stopped by the station to say our good byes. We were given lots of hugs and smiles. I asked the mother hen if she was ready to talk and she said not yet. The ride to the airport was long and I was tired. I wanted to go home to see my family and process the last week in this place where tragedy had struck. The city girl and I stood there at the airport and it appeared the tornado of emotions that put us together had stopped. We talked about the last week and we were no longer strangers, we now had become friends.

My wife said our boys wanted to surprise me and greet me at the airport and I said ok. When the wheels landed on the ground the vortex of emotions that surrounded me had returned. I acted surprised when my boys ran from behind a staircase and hugged me but what was not a surprise were the tears that gushed from my eyes.

The next day I was back in the woods with my rifle pressed against my cheek and I did my best to place that round through that quarter, sometimes our best is all we have to give. I continued to shoot until I was at my best and placed a USMC key chain at 200 yards. I pressed my cheek against the stock, found my sweet spot, controlled my breathing, thought about those men and women who gave it all and focused on the task at hand. I placed two rounds through the key chain. The next day the key chain was mailed to the city girl, she earned it.

I stayed in contact with the old devil dog's daughter and she kept me advised of his progress. She praised me for what I did for her father that, in my opinion, was nothing. She said he was a different man than before that day and I had something to do with that. Once again, in my opinion, I did nothing.

Time slipped by and I soon realized it had been one year since that day. As the wheels landed on the ground I found myself once again back in that vortex of emotions. The city girl pulled up to the airport curb and we were off to that place. We drove into a field and parked the car. I told the city girl not to step in the cow poop. We walked towards a large metal shelter with lots of people under it. Before I could move towards the old devil dog he came at me like a bullet. I had not seen him in a year and had not spoken to him since I left. He hugged me hard and his wife and the mother hen were soon to follow. I sat next to him and I reached in my pocket and pulled out my dad's medals. I said, "You can hold these for the memorial service but I get them back" and he said, "Ok." As the anniversary memorial service proceeded he leaned over and said, "I'm talking to someone about that day and Vietnam." I said, "Did we teach an old dog new tricks?" He said, "No, it was just time." I asked about his son. He said "My son really stepped up to the challenge when I was down and I'm proud of him."

The next day the city girl and I presented the old devil dog with something to remember us by. His whole family and the mother hen were present. I said, "Few things in life are an honor, it was an honor to walk across the parade deck of Parris Island to become a Marine, it was an honor to watch my wife give birth to our boys, it was an honor to tell my father he was going to die. The problem is people like you feel that you burden us when you tell us about your bad day, but in reality it is a privilege and an honor to hear about your bad day".

We returned to station to see a few more people. I saw the Dutchman who still had his quarter on his keychain. I saw the fixer who had no issues looking at me and talking to me and he also still had his USMC key chain. I walked into the office and found the mother hen being a mother hen. I handed her a small toy rabbit. Then I told her a story about a guy I worked with who told me his story about another bad event where the only thing that survived was a rabbit. I said, "I'm not sure why the rabbit survived and you are just like the rabbit, you survived." The yearlong tears broke from her eyes and she told me her story. I hugged her and said, "Who are you?" She said, "The rabbit." The fire station no longer looked like one of my dad's beehives. The queen had returned and the worker bees had their leader back.

Our last stop was the old devil dog's house. The city girl and I hugged him and his wife. We thanked them for being so kind to us but they praised us for what we did. I hugged the old devil dog one more time and said I love you and he said I love you too. My dad died when I was 43 and I never recall him telling me he loved me, but I also never recall me telling him I loved him.

Once again the city girl and I stood at the airport watching the vortex of emotions disappear into the air. We are honored and blessed to come together when tragedy strikes in hopes we can help those involved move forward. Our recent trip validated the need for people like us. I often say no special skills needed for this job, just show up.

It's too windy today to punch a quarter at 300 yards so I'm stuck here at 100 yards. I just punched four holes in a quarter and I know my dad is loving that. What started out as a special thing for my dad on a hillside farm many years ago has now turned into something unexpected. I would love to think that I will never give another hole-punched quarter to a person hurting but as long as there is a human race there will be tragedy. Tragedies define us and if we let them they can destroy us. In a small town in the middle of nowhere tragedy struck and they will not allow that to destroy them. Men and women gave their best. Some died. Some survived. The answers we seek in order to understand tragedies sometimes are not there. We do know tragedy brings us together, teaches old dogs news tricks, teaches young dogs to say I love you even when it might be too late, and tragedy is the best teacher of letting us know how strong we really are.

My father's medals are lying next to my rifle as I look through the scope. His medals inspire me to continue this work and not question why I was chosen to look over those caskets or have the honor to be a part of the aftermath as we as a race continue to have days like that day. His medals are tarnished and that reminds me that no matter how hard we try some things we cannot wash from our bodies, our minds, our souls, and our hearts, but again worn and weathered defines who we are. His medals remind me of his physical pain and my emotional pain and how important it is to believe that the next day will be better than that day.

– WLV –

Crisis Concepts and Precepts

Lesson 6
"Crisis Intervention Steps"

Steps-by-Step approach to Crisis Intervention

Caution: It is helpful to have models and step-by-step procedures to assist us in providing CISM services. They help us to organize our approach to distressed people. They help us to think clearly. Crisis Support, however, should never be rigid, rushed, or thoughtless. Step-by-step procedures should guide us, not dictate to us. Common sense, innovation, flexibility, and strategic thinking will have more positive effects than unbending adherence to rules and steps. Please, use Crisis Intervention steps as guidelines.

In the previous story the agents assisting the fire personnel had a very complex situation on their hands. There were multiple line-of-duty deaths and a number of the personnel had trauma in their backgrounds. The step-by-step procedures were present in the backdrop, but the agents used a considerable amount of innovation, such as Josey's use of the quarters, key chains and medals, to break down barriers and gain trust.

No one should expect instantaneous acceptance by people in a crisis. Likewise, do not expect that CISM will have immediate effects. It takes time and patience. Sometimes, suggestions are made and, analogously, seeds are planted. At some time later, results may be perceived. In the case of the story in Chapter 6, it was a year before some of the people opened up to support personnel. Attempting to force that willingness to accept support would never have worked. When providing crisis support, keep your expectations under control.

The other side of helping people is that there are times when you feel as though you did very little or nothing. Yet those seemingly small efforts yield very positive results, sometimes to our surprise.

All that being said, let us now look at the steps in crisis work.

Steps in Crisis Intervention

(Adapted from the work of Dr. Albert Roberts, Crisis Intervention Handbook, Assessment, Treatment and Research, 2005.)

1. **Introduction**. It is extremely important that crisis workers and support personnel introduce themselves and explain briefly their role in the situation. Use the introduction to perform a preliminary assessment of the person and the situation. Listen carefully to how the distressed person answers your questions. Obtain the names and relationships of people you are currently helping. Also, be sure to obtain the names and contact information of the people you are attempting to assist.

2. **Assess situation and impact on the people involved.** Assessment should cover the nature and

magnitude of the event plus the level of impact on the personnel. The incident or situation is certainly important, but the reactions of the personnel are even more important. Ask about what happened, their reactions, and what may be the aspects that are most bothersome.

3. **Mentally list all possible options.** As you assess the nature and magnitude of the event and the impact on the people involved, you should begin to make a mental list of the possible options to manage the crisis reactions. Some of those mental options may be employed to reduce the distress and move toward crisis resolution. By making this mental list of options, you begin to develop a crisis action plan.

4. **Choose best option.** Start by asking the person or people involved in the situation if they know what might help them. Some options mentioned by those involved may be worthwhile. If the person is uncertain as to what to do, then you should draw from you mental list some potential actions that might help. Find something that the person is willing to try. Together you develop a *crisis action plan* and prepare to set that plan in motion.

5. **Implement the best option immediately**. After developing a crisis action plan, get some action going immediately. Focusing on carrying out a plan helps the person to regain control and reduce anxiety.

6. **Reassess**. Once action has begun, monitor the progress of the individual or group receiving assistance.

7. **Maintain, change, abandon the option.** If the plan appears to be having positive effects, keep it going. Some plans may need to be altered. If the goals of the intervention have been achieved, the plan may be abandoned.

8. **Closure of intervention.** Two or three things may end a crisis intervention procedure. *First*, the person you are trying to help may reject your efforts. You cannot force your help on anyone. See if the person will accept help from someone else. If not, express you concern for the distressed person, wish them well, and say goodbye. *Second*, you are transferring the person or group to another level of care (hospital, law enforcement agency, other family members, etc.) You should inform the receiving parties about what has happened to the person and what has been done so far. You may also make additional suggestions. Acknowledge the person you were assisting; ask if they need any additional support from you. Then provide reassurance and encouragement and say goodbye. *Third*, in some cases, the crisis work that you did was sufficient. All indications suggest that they can handle the situation on their own. Let them know that you see noticeable improvements. You believe they can handle things from this point forward. If they agree, provide contact information in case they need additional assistance. Wish them well and say goodbye. Let them know that you will be following up in a few days just to make sure things are working out okay.

NOTE: One exception. If the person you are dealing with is suicidal, you must make sure that they are transferred to appropriate professional care even if they try to reject your help. You cannot leave suicidal people alone. You must engage others to be helpful in the situation. The aim for crisis workers when dealing with a suicidal person is to get others involved in the helping process.

Chapter 7

Damp Boots

In the 1950's, a child was born to a hillside farm family in the back wood hills of Missouri. The child's name was Norris. Norris's adolescent years were spent like most kids growing up on a farm. When he was not working on the farm he could be found hunting in the woods. Around the end of his teenage years Norris made the decision to join the military. Unlike most teenagers Norris became a man overnight. He had no idea that his decision would impact the rest of his life.

In the fall of 1994, I had the pleasure of meeting Norris. Norris and I had mutual friends, so I had heard plenty of stories about him. I heard that Norris was a good old country boy and was, for the most part, a quiet person. Some said Norris did not care about tomorrow, he just lived for today. I had also heard that Norris could have done great things with his life but had chosen not to. Some people thought he had wasted his life and had a bad attitude. As Norris stepped out of his truck on that fall day in 1994, I could see his long cowboy mustache from where I was standing. He was wearing blue jeans and cowboy boots. He wore a baseball cap that looked like it could use a good bath. I guess from a distance we looked like two male dogs getting ready to fight. I introduced myself and we shook hands. He had a firm handshake and his hand was as rough as sandpaper. Right away I knew this man did not have a bad attitude but something in his life had given him an edge. I looked into his eyes and it was like looking into a bottomless pit. For being a young man, he had a lot of traveled miles in his eyes.

Over the next year, Norris and I became good friends. He was a quiet person and did not talk much about himself. I have always believed that if someone wants you to know something about him or her, he or she will tell you. So with me being this way, I guess our friendship worked really well for Norris. Norris cared a lot about people and would help anyone that gave him the opportunity. I knew Norris for a year but I still did not know much about him. In the fall of 1995, I was offered a job on the East Coast. I told Norris about the job and he replied, "Don't give them your heart." I thought about asking Norris what that meant but I knew he would not tell me the answer.

I took the job on the East Coast and the first place I visited was the Vietnam Memorial. When I was growing up, I could never understand why the history books in school only had two pages on Vietnam. All the other wars had several pages but not the Vietnam War. I asked the history teacher why and I did not receive a good answer. I then asked the teacher why killing in a war wasn't breaking the "thou shall not kill" commandment. The teacher replied, "God makes exceptions for war." As I looked at the wall I saw a lot of exceptions. I stayed in contact with Norris and we actually became better friends even with the greater distance between us.

My new job was not what I thought it would be and I missed having someone to relate to. I decided to have

Norris out for a visit, so I bought a plane ticket and mailed it to him. As I saw Norris walk across the airport lobby, he brought a smile to my face. I shook his sandpaper hand and he said, "Last time I was on a plane was when I came back from Vietnam."

We had known each other for over two years and that was the first time he mentioned the war. Someone told me once that Norris was in the war but I never asked him. The next morning I told Norris I had a surprise for him. We drove down to the Vietnam Memorial and walked over to the wall. I looked into Norris's eyes. The bottomless pit was replaced by a distant land he had tried to forget.. That distant land was in front of him in the shape of a wall. I asked Norris if he wanted me to walk with him and he said, "Maybe I'll do this one on my own." I went over to some trees about 100 yards from the wall and watched him as he walked. The edge that some people mistook for an attitude was slowly crumbling away. As Norris walked it appeared that his posture was disappearing. He stopped along the wall at several spots and just stood there. As he stared into the wall, it appeared from where I was standing that Norris was nothing more than an old feeble man. Norris made his way over to a park bench and slumped over with his hands holding his face. I could tell from where I was standing that Norris's whole body was shaking from his crying. I reached up and wiped the tears from my eyes. Now I knew what he meant when he said, "Don't give them your heart." Even though my friend's name was not on this wall, his heart was.

Norris sat on the bench for a long time and then walked over to me. I did not say a word and neither did Norris. We walked back to the car and drove to my house. As I drove Norris told me his story. After high school he joined the military. Norris was sent to Vietnam. He said it was a long way from the Missouri hills. He said he knew when he joined the military that he would be sent to Vietnam. Norris said it was something he had to do. The country boy in Norris made him an ideal soldier. The only difference now was he was hunting the invisible man. Norris said that he soon realized this was much different than hunting a buck deer on a ridge top in Missouri. He told me that he soon figured out that the only way to survive was to fill his soul with hate. I had heard the word hate before but after that day, the word never sounded the same to me. He told me that hate had become easy for him. That scared him more than the war. He told me in the quiet times he would dream of going home but in his soul there was still a war going on. Norris said that Vietnam was very different from Missouri. The fields were not safe to run across. The woods were not safe to walk through. Most of all, he said his boots were always damp.

He said he separated his heart from his soul and just did what he was told. The hate took over his soul and he found a way to survive. He said you can't imagine what it is like to wake up everyday and all you want to do is go home. The fear you feel is for everything. Never before had he felt fear for an empty field of grass, or a patch of woods. But in this place a piece of metal the size of a pencil eraser was just one more thing you feared. During his entire childhood, Norris was the hunter but now he was just like the buck deer.

Much of what Norris said to me explained a lot about the person he had become. As I drove, I just sat there and listened to his story. As Norris continued to talk about the war I could see the hate coming out of him. His hands were clenched and his face had become flushed with anger. He said that every day was the same and soon all he could do was hate. Norris never did say how long he was in Vietnam and, as usual, I did not ask. I never asked Norris what he did or did not do. It really does not matter to me. What matters most is that he survived. My friend found himself in a situation and he did what he had to do to survive. To a soldier in the field wearing damp boots the war is not about winning, but about surviving and coming home.

Norris said he was offered an opportunity after his time in Vietnam to do something else for the military but turned it down. Norris just wanted to go home. Norris said he was not mad that he did not receive a parade and that most people hated him for being in the war. He said that when he stepped off the plane and felt home and in dry boots, that was all the thanks he needed. He was alive and was home. After his dry boots touched American soil it was time to become the boy he had left behind.

Norris said the transition was not that easy but the hard part was finding a place for all that hate. Norris said, "When I hate, I hate real bad." As fast as he had become angry he calmed down. He looked over at me and said, "I am going to burn in hell for what I did over there." I replied, "God makes exceptions for war." It was the only answer I could think of. A few days later Norris flew back to Missouri and we never talked about the war again.

It has been several years since that day and I once again have moved on to a different job. I left my East Coast job because I feared I would give them my heart. After seeing what giving your heart can do to someone, I realized I was headed down that road. There is not a day that goes by that I am not troubled by my friend's belief in where his soul will go. I have never been in combat, or in a war. For those who have, I thank you. I fail to see how some can judge those in war, when they are not in their damp boots. All they want to do is come home. When soldiers have to forget what their God has taught them, and then they are placed in a situation where no rules apply, no wonder some get lost in the confusion. Whatever Norris did in that place called Vietnam, I will not judge his actions or reactions.

As for Norris, I understand him a lot better now. He is just happy to be home. He lives for today and hopes he will see tomorrow. Now he spends his days helping people, raising his family, and he does it wearing dry boots. He lives down the road from his mom and dad and helps them as they grow older. As the sun sets in the Missouri hills you can see Norris walking across a grassy field. He doesn't watch his step and the earth under his dry boots is home. As he sits down under an oak tree, he pulls out his pocket knife and cleans the American soil out from under his finger nails.

I think of Norris often and wish I could convince him he will not burn in hell. If Norris is right and he is going to hell for the things he did in that place called Vietnam, then hell is full of a lot of good people. I wrote this story for Norris and anyone who did what they had to do to survive. I pray that I will never have to wear damp boots but if do I will wear them with pride. My generation has forgotten about veterans and people who fought the good fight. I wish my generation and those who judge others could have been there that day with me as I saw my friend crumble before me eyes. Maybe then they would understand that just because someone does something outside what we are taught as children, it does not mean they are no longer human. I still do not have an answer to my childhood question, why killing in war wasn't breaking the "thou shall not kill" commandment. Hopefully, when my children look up to me and ask me that same question I can say something better than; "God makes exceptions for war".

Written by a friend

- WLV -

Crisis Concepts and Precepts

Lesson 7
"Posttraumatic Stress Disorder"

Notes on Norris: The description of Norris' actions and reactions at the Vietnam Memorial Wall in Chapter 7 leads to the reasonable conclusion that Norris is most likely suffering from Posttraumatic Stress Disorder (PTSD). We can only say 'most likely' because PTSD cannot be officially diagnosed without a professional evaluation. The story provides many of the tell-tail signs, however, and a reasonable conclusion of PTSD is justified.

PTSD is the cause of intense and prolonged suffering and disruption to normal life experiences. A main factor in the development of PTSD is exposure to overwhelming and threatening traumatic stress. War is not the only cause of PTSD, but it is certainly one of the most common ones. The starting point for PTSD is the exposure to or the direct experience of a critical incident. A critical incident is a horrible, terrible, awful, overwhelming, threatening, frightening, terrifying, or grotesque event. It causes *Critical Incident Stress* as described below. If the critical incident stress is resolved, the person is left with a painful memory. It is when the critical incident stress cannot be resolved that PTSD develops. That can turn into a life-long disruptive and painful condition.

Critical Incident Stress is extremely common after people are exposed to traumatic events. It is a normal, healthy response of normal people to a terribly abnormal event. Some level of distress is expected for the majority of people faced with events that are grotesque, threatening, overwhelming, or frightening. Most people experience the distress and then they bounce-back after some time and resume normal life functions. Another name for Critical Incident Stress is "Post Traumatic Stress." It should not to be confused with Post Traumatic Stress Disorder (described below). When Critical Incident Stress is managed well people tend to recover. When it is not managed and some resolution is not found, it may turn into one or more of a number of conditions associated with the exposure to a traumatic event. For example exposure to traumatic stress can result in depression, brief psychotic reaction, panic attacks, substance abuse, withdrawal from others, rage reactions, changes in personality and Post Traumatic Stress Disorder. The worst of these conditions is Post Traumatic Stress Disorder (PTSD). The story of Norris in chapter 7 strongly suggests that he is suffering from at least a moderate level of PTSD.

Post Traumatic Stress Disorder (PTSD)

PTSD is an anxiety disorder that occurs when people have been exposed to horrible events that are generally outside of the realm of circumstances normally encountered by human beings. The events are so shocking, overwhelming, and disorienting that the person is unable to recover and resume normal life activities and behaviors. Their emotions are out of control and difficult to endure. It is as if a switch inside them is flipped and it gets stuck in the "on" position.

PTSD Rates

PTSD depends on the nature and intensity of exposure to the horrible event and, most importantly, the personal view of the event. About 80% of Americans are exposed to a traumatic event in their lives, but only about 9% develop PTSD. The more personally threatening the traumatic experience is perceived to be, the greater the impact on the person experiencing it. Sexual assault victims, for instance, develop PTSD at a rate between 40 and 70%. Victims of torture or terrorism have PTSD rates ranging between 40 and 90%. The more they felt that their lives were in immediate danger, the greater the likelihood that they developed PTSD.

Criteria for PTSD

1. Exposure to actual or threatened death, serious injury, sexual violence. Combat certainly fits in this category.
2. One or more symptoms of intrusion (repeatedly seeing it, hearing it, smelling it, tasting it or feeling it) associated with the traumatic event.
3. Persistent avoidance of stimuli of the traumatic event, beginning after the traumatic event.
4. Negative alteration in thoughts and feelings associated with the traumatic event and beginning or worsening after the traumatic event.
5. Noticeably increased arousal and reactions associated with the traumatic event that began after the exposure to the traumatic event. Symptoms of arousal include sleeplessness, restlessness, loss of attention and concentration, inability to relax and hyper alertness.
6. The duration of the symptoms of distress (2, 3, 4, 5

above) last longer than one month.

7. Significant distress and changes in social, occupational, and other normal life activities.

8. The disturbances described in the points above are not the result of substances such as medication, drugs, or alcohol nor are they associated with other medical conditions.

Healing After PTSD

The intensity of PTSD can be mild, moderate, or severe. When it is mild, the person will fulfill most of the criteria in the list above and the experience of PTSD will be distressing and uncomfortable. He or she may have disturbing dreams and fairly strong reactions to stimuli. The symptoms, however, do not stop the person from working and living relatively normally. In some cases, the person may gradually experience a diminishing of the symptoms. It is possible that a slow, but spontaneous recovery may occur even without professional help.

When PTSD is moderate in intensity, the person suffers from many more intense symptoms. When the condition is severe, life's functions are often difficult or impossible to conduct. Severe PTSD can often lead to significant substance abuse and entry into hospital settings for the treatment of medical and psychiatric conditions that may accompany the PTSD.

There are many things a person can do to help him or herself. People are certainly encouraged to take control of their own healing. No one should leave his own recovery up to someone else. Each person with PTSD must be the master of his own care.

Here are some things that may help:

- Stress management education
- Psychological evaluation
- PTSD education
- Peer support
- Professional care / treatment
- The right therapy program
- Talking to trusted people
- Reduce negative thinking
- Practicing calming techniques
- Rest / sleep
- PTSD is a fairly common reaction. You are not alone.
- Physical activity
- Motivation to recover
- Eliminate feelings of shame
- PTSD is not something a person chooses
- Many have recovered from PTSD. Join them.
- PTSD results form circumstances outside of the person, not from some internal weakness

If the PTSD is moderate or severe, it is most likely that people are going to need professional assistance. It is critical to a person's recovery that a qualified mental health professional be involved as early as possible in the healing and recovery process. The passage of time without appropriate assistance will typically make the recovery process longer and more complicated.

Therapies For PTSD

No one therapy is known to be successful for every person with PTSD. People are different and have different needs and they will respond more to one type of therapy than to another. Sometimes combinations or blends of therapies can be very helpful.

Behavioral Therapy (BT) helps a person to gain control over the physical reactions associated with PTSD. It focuses on relaxation training, biofeedback and systematic desensitization.

Cognitive Behavioral Therapy (CBT) helps a person to understand the personal meanings behind the traumatic experience. It challenges facts and beliefs. It pairs new thoughts with the trauma. It decreases symptoms.

Eye Movement Desensitization and Reprocessing (EMDR) helps the brain complete processing of the trauma. The therapist guides the person through a series of eye movements. The therapy has a very positive record.

Trauma Incident Reduction (TIR) utilizes multiple repetitions of the trauma story. The person gains more control and the symptoms lessen.

Some people with PTSD also experienced a violent blow and might have *traumatic brain injury* (TBI) that needs medical evaluation and care. Please do not self-care. Get help for PTSD and TBI.

Chapter 8

If Only

"Your flight is delayed, Sir," said the smiling ticket agent. I asked, "How long a delay." "About three hours," she quickly said and never even lost the smile. My shoulders sank. I was tired after days of teaching and just wanted to go home. Being quite early for a flight that was delayed three hours did not help.

The gate area was empty. I thought that was a good thing. When I talk for four days, I really do not want to talk to anyone. I thought I would just wait it out and catch up on reading.

An elderly gentleman walked into the gate area and came over to where I was sitting. *Oh no*, I thought. *There were forty-nine chairs to choose from and he is coming over here. I just want to be alone and read.*

He said, "Hi, I'm Phil. I was at the other gate. My flight is delayed. You delayed too?" I nodded. He asked if he could sit down. I nodded in the affirmative again. I did not want to be discourteous to Phil. He asked, "Who are you?" I answered, "I'm Jeff." "Great, Jeff, what do you do?"

I thought to myself, "Maybe I should just tell him what I do. Most people would not want to hear that I am mental health professional with unusual interests and they pull

75

away." I gave him the short version. I told him that I worked with terrible things, disasters, baby deaths, gloom and doom, blood and guts, and pain and gore.

Phil looked at me with an unreadable, faraway look. Then he said quietly, "I was in a disaster once." I felt a bit guilty for my abrupt introduction earlier. My curiosity soared. "Which one?" He told me that we just were about a week past the anniversary. I blurted out, "Coconut Grove Fire, Boston, Massachusetts, November 28, 1942," like I was a contestant in a TV game show. He gazed at me and said, "How did you know that?" "It is what I do," I responded. "I am specialist in disasters." He said, "I was there. It was horrible. I have lived it everyday of my life since it happened." I told him I was sorry and went silent.

My new companion launched into a detailed description of the Coconut Grove tragedy from start to horrible conclusion. It was as if I had flipped a switch and he went into an autopilot mode. He talked non-stop. I did not have to say anything and he had my full attention.

He, his date, and four friends went to enjoy dinner and an evening of entertainment and dancing. The Coconut Grove was very crowed that night. After a customer complaint about how dark it was by his table, a bus boy attempted to change a recessed ceiling light bulb by the light of a Zippo lighter. In an instant, ceiling decorations were burning and flaming particles were dropping on tablecloths, furnishings, and carpeting, setting new fires. He thought it was like the ceiling was burning and melting because flaming drops kept falling off the ceiling. My companion described how he grabbed the hand of his date and told his friends to follow him because he was getting her out. Flames were growing rapidly and thickening smoke was everywhere.

Survivors poured out of the front doors of the burning structure. It was a slow process, however, because there were revolving doors and too many people trying to get out through the same exit. It was growing hotter and the smoke was making it difficult to breathe. Some people were panicking and pushing others. Some went toward chained and locked rear and side doors and were trapped and crushed by the weight of those pushing from behind. Phil led his girl out through the open but crowded entry doors. He gripped her wrist tightly and would not let go. They were choking and coughing when they got outside. Phil said he coughed for months after the fire.

Waiting anxiously outside in the cold, the couple watched as firefighters entered the building and fought back the flames. They kept looking for their friends as people came out in less and less numbers. For a while, clouds of smoke poured out of the building. It wasn't too long before the flames were beaten out and the smoke became much lighter. There was still no sign of their friends. Police officers and fire personnel approached and said, "You guys in uniform, we need some help getting the victims out." My storyteller joined the effort. He told me, "You could not say 'no.' You were in uniform and you could not be a coward. You felt you had an obligation to do something that might help. I thought if I went in, I might find my friends and lead them out." He found his friends, but they were dead. He helped some soldiers and firefighters remove bodies. "After a while, we ran out of space on the sidewalk. A fire officer said we needed to stack them on top of each other. There were almost five hundred bodies that we brought out. I had a hard time dealing with those awful scenes that night. I can still see them in my mind today." He was chocked up and tearing. I asked him if he would prefer not to go on with the story. He answered that he really wanted to tell the whole story and he continued.

The story was spellbinding. I listened intensely to Phil as the time sped by. It was the fastest three hours I had ever experienced. He cried during parts of the story especially when he described his friends and the young people who were crushed at the locked exit doors and the stacks of bodies outside. Some died at their tables as if they were unaware of the threats they faced.

Phil was just wrapping up the final details of his story when they announced that his flight was boarding. He concluded his comments, gathered his things and stood up to leave. I stood and thanked him for sharing his powerful story. I put my hand out to shake his hand. He pulled me toward himself and put his arms around me and hugged me tight. He said, "I wish I had been able to talk to you after the fire. This is the first time in 50 years that I have ever been able to tell the whole story. I feel like a thousand pounds are off my shoulders. They told us after the war to put all the horror behind us and not talk about it. They said that nobody would understand or listen to all that painful stuff. If only there was someone like you, I would not have had to dream about it every night for 50 years. Thank you."

- JTM -

Crisis Concepts and Precepts

Lesson 8
"The Human Brain, Trauma, and Hamster Wheels "

The Human Brain and Traumatic Experiences

The human brain is a remarkable organ. Its capacity to process and remember facts, and to analyze and synthesize a wide range of inputs is extraordinary beyond description.

The brain has several memory systems. One is the kinesthetic memory system in which a vast array of movements and the coordination of muscle groups are maintained. Without kinesthetic memory we would not remember how to walk when we woke up in the morning. Of course, all other movement functions of the human body would cease as well. Another memory system is the general memory system in which the brain processes and stores a staggering amount of information over the life span of a person. Finally there is an emergency memory system. This system remembers facts, information, emotions, thoughts, and bodily functions that are critical to survival. It is into this memory system in the brain that traumatic experiences are logged and connected with the reflexive physical systems of the body. The emergency memory system allows us to instantaneously recognize threats, and to take immediate evasive actions or to go into an acute state of arousal so that we can take effective actions to defend our family members or ourselves.

There are several things, besides having several memory systems, which the brain can do exceptionally well.

Complete

First the brain tries to complete every experience. When we look at Roman ruins, the brain tries to conger up images of how it all looked in the glory days of ancient Rome. When we watch a mystery movie, the brain tries very hard to conclude who did the crime before the movie lets us know the ending. It is the same way when we are involved in building a puzzle. The brain works especially hard to mentally assemble the pieces before our hands actually put the pieces together.

In a traumatic experience, the human brain is trying to make sense out of chaos. It tries to complete the experience by imagining a different, but better outcome. It tries to fill in missing details. The brain attempts to complete the experience by gathering enough details from memories of the event to bring a criminal subject to justice. It is not always successful, but the brain will keep trying for completeness for however long it takes, even if that turns out to be a lifetime.

Simplify

The human brain is a highly complex organ, but it is especially proficient at simplifying things. It tries to reduce experiences to simple causes and effects. If a violent act is committed against a loved one, the brain, being oriented toward simplicity, will help the person to think, "I went to work, therefore my wife was vulnerable to assault and someone attacked her. Therefore, it is all my fault." Another example would be a firefighter who traded shifts with a friend who is assigned to the same engine. The friend is killed and the firefighter then feels he caused the death of his friend by trading shifts. The simplification does not have to be accurate, but the brain is satisfied when it makes the experience simple.

Categorize

A third powerful feature of the human brain is that it attempts to categorize every experience and every event that humans encounter in their lives. The brain makes categories to assist in the retrieval of information and memories. There are categories for family, friends, work, events, pleasures, pain, body systems, subjects, tools, equipment, movements, disappointments, dreams, wishes, fears, frustrations and so on. The brain always tries to put things in a category. Always.

Hamster Wheels

Severe traumatic events do not fit very well in to the standard categories that our brains have been able to establish in the course of the previous experiences in our lives. The brain, however, keeps trying to categorize even when we do not have a category.

In a sense, it is like a hamster in a wheel. A hamster keeps going and going around and around in the hamster wheel but they he never gets anywhere.

When our brains can't categorize a traumatic experience, we climb inside our internal hamster wheels and we keep going around and around trying to find meaning for the traumatic experience and a place to categorize the event in our minds.

In the story in Chapter 8, Phil dreams of the horrors of losing four friends in the Coconut Grove fire, when he and his date barely escaped alive. Then, to make the traumatic experience even worse, Phil helps remove a number of the bodies of the deceased. He has repeated exposures to the horrific scenes both inside and outside of the club. His mind is overloaded by the horror and his brain cannot deal with it nor can it find meaning or a proper category. In what kind of a category do you place a near death experience, the loss of four friends on the same night, and repeated exposure to nearly 500 deceased young people? Phil was in his own hamster wheel for half a century.

Keep this adage in mind "A trauma or a crisis remains a trauma or a crisis until some resolution is found."

Chapter 9

Billy's Last Ride

I sat on my banana seat bike as my father taped two pieces of pipe on the frame to make it look like exhaust pipes on a motorcycle. My father stood up and said that I was "good to go." I pushed my bike to the top of the hill in our yard as my dad stood at the bottom of the hill and waited for me. I crawled up on the bike and sat there looking at my dad. He yelled, "Bring it on," and I rolled off the hill. I was half way down the hill and hit a bump and landed at his feet. My dad picked me up as tears squeezed out of the corners of my eyes. He told me that Billy the Kid would not cry and he dusted me off. I was wearing my favorite Billy the Kid denim jacket that was now covered in grass and dirt. I never cried because Billy the Kid would not have.

After I turned 21, I decided to take my Jeep to my first job interview in law enforcement since it was March and it would be a little warmer than my Harley. As I drove 15 miles down the curvy black top road, the soft-top in my CJ5 whipped in the wind. Between the soft-top whipping and the dual exhaust from the V8 engine I could not hear the radio, but I was riding in style. I pulled up to the sheriff's task force office and headed up the stairs to my interview. I was interviewing for a position on the local drug task force that was being run by a Lieutenant with the sheriff's office. I had a two-year degree in law enforcement but had never been a police officer. I had just turned 21 but I looked like I was 14. I was told because I looked so young I would be good for undercover work. I entered the Lieutenant's (Lt.) office. Before long the sheriff entered and asked a few questions and I was offered the job. I was handed a badge and gun but told to leave the badge at home. I was also told to not tell anyone what I was doing to include my parents, my girlfriend, and anyone else that mattered. My job was simple, go to bars, meet people, and buy dope. At that time in Missouri you could be a police officer without attending the police academy for up to one year. The academy was three weeks long.

As I rode home I tried to figure out what the hell I was going to tell my parents that I was now doing for a living. I came up with the idea that I was working security for a man who owned a bunch of gas stations. My parents seem to buy the story and that was what I told everyone.

My first night in the bar was hard. I did not drink or smoke, but I was a people person. My Lt. was a good man but knew little about working cold undercover (no informants). After several weeks I felt like a total failure because I had not bought any dope.

I went into the Lt.'s office one day and he had a guy in his office who looked like a bad guy. The Lt. introduced me to Billy (his undercover name). Billy was a state trooper who was assigned to the narcotics section of the highway patrol; he was a legend in the undercover world. I had heard plenty of stories about Billy at the local junior college. Billy looked at me, said hi, and then said, "You look like a Kid." Billy asked about a guy that I was trying to buy dope from and he said if you buy some dope from him, I will buy you a steak dinner. I left the Lt.'s office on cloud nine and I knew no matter what, I had to make a buy from the guy so Billy would respect me.

I tried for weeks to get next to the guy in the bar but could never make a connection. The guy owned a used car lot, so I took my 79 CJ5 Jeep to the guy and asked him if he would buy it. He bought my Jeep and we became friends. It killed me to sell my Jeep. My mom had made leather seat covers for it and my best friend had welded some metal into the floor to seal the rust holes but I wanted Billy to buy me that steak dinner.

As the weeks pressed on Billy and I became friends, he was not the typical police officer I was used to. Billy would sit for hours in front of his television watching the Three Stooges and laugh so hard he would cry. Billy was very rough on the outside but he was very compassionate, and then he had a side that would go to hell to protect you. I admired Billy and in many ways he had become my law enforcement father. A few weeks passed and I finally made a buy from the guy that owned the car lot. Billy never bought me a steak but I had earned his respect. From that point forward I was known as "The Kid."

Billy had a fellow trooper friend visit one week and he too worked in narcotics. His name was Jesse and he was nothing like the laid back, funny Billy, but Billy assured me he was a good guy. I respected Jesse but I did not care for him, he was not like Billy.

Once I needed to go somewhere but did not have a vehicle. Rarely do Harley riders let someone else ride their bikes, but Billy said I was ok and that was enough for Jesse. On Billy's word, Jesse let me borrow his Harley.

Over the next year I learned much from Billy, some of it was about being a good undercover agent and some of it was about not making the mistakes he did. Most guys who lived undercover had a partner, I never did. I guess that was why Billy gave me so much attention. He knew how hard it was to adapt to that way of living. It could be a very lonely life.

After a year, Jesse offered me a job working for him on a state task force. Billy said it was a great opportunity, so I took the job. I was not thrilled about working for Jesse but Billy reassured me that he was a good guy. I trusted Billy's judgment. I loaded up the car and Billy drove me three hours to Jesse's house. Jesse was not home and was running late, which is standard procedure for a narc. Billy dropped me off, I watched him drive off and I hated him for leaving me. I sat on the curb until Jesse came home. He tried to be nice but he was still nothing like Billy.

Jesse set me up in an undercover apartment. The investigation could last for as long as year and a half. I was three hours from home and an hour from Jesse's house. I felt like a solider being dropped behind enemy lines but I was alone. Jesse did his best to help me adapt. I would call Billy and talk about quitting but he would encourage me to stick with it. I would tell Billy how much I disliked Jesse but he assured me he was a good guy. Billy came to visit me a few times and it was nice to have someone in my apartment who knew who I really was. His visits were short. He encouraged me to stick with it. Being three hours from Billy forced me to rely on Jesse and his knowledge of living undercover. Jesse's advice was always very direct and serious. The big difference between Billy and Jesse was Billy would manipulate me to get me to do something and Jesse would just ride my ass until I did it.

It took about six months for me to finally find that side of Jesse that Billy had told me about. Jesse would come to visit me in my undercover apartment and we would talk for hours. Jesse also would force me to come and spend the night at his house just to give me a reality check. His wife and daughter treated me like family and I needed that.

Jesse would take me to crack houses from time to time when they needed to make some crack buys in order to get enough probable cause for a search warrant. I always looked forward to those trips with Jesse; it was a nice break from being alone. He would drop me off down the street and tell me that if I was not out in 10 minutes his truck would be coming through the front door, so move out of the way. I knew he was serious and the side Billy talked about came out more and more.

After two years of living with criminals I finally reached the point that it was easier to live with the criminals than go home and be the real me. I once had a conversation with Billy about living the two lives and he said, "Kid the best time is when you are between your real home and your undercover home." I asked why and he said, "Because you can't do anything about either one, all you can do is ride; it's a peaceful place to be." I knew what I was doing was not good for my state of mind but I was much better at my job if I just lived in one world. People on the outside could never understand that if you left your undercover life for more than a few days your criminal friends would suspect you had been arrested and were talking. When you returned after a few days it was like starting all over. Even though I was alone, I was glad I was not like Billy and Jesse who had families. In order for their investigations to be a success they had to choose the criminals over their loved ones.

Years later, I felt my pager vibrate in my front pocket as I sat in a tree blind, hunting. It was my wife paging me. I reached into my camouflaged cargo pocket and removed my cell phone and called my wife. My wife told me that Jesse had just called and Billy had been in a motorcycle wreck, Billy was still alive but it was over. I told my wife I would be home in a few. I sat there, 25 feet off the ground with every thought, feeling and emotion running through my head like a bullet. I could smell the swamp more than ever. The air was humid and hot but I was cold. A tear squeezed from my eye and landed on my rifle but soon disappeared. I climbed down from the tree and let the dark waters of the swamp surround my rubber boots. I walked the mile back to my Jeep and thought about how long it had been since I had seen Billy. I left Missouri in 1995 and remember seeing Billy in 1997 but could not recall anytime since then.

By the time I made it back to the Jeep I was soaked in sweat from the May heat but I was still cold. When I got home I called Jesse who told me Billy and the boys were on a cancer motorcycle benefit ride and Billy lost control on a four-lane highway. Jesse said Billy was still alive but only because of the machines he was hooked up to. I told Jesse to keep me posted. I walked into the kitchen and my wife said she was sorry and I said I know.

I walked into our home office where I have a wall full of 8X10 pictures of those years of working under cover. There is a picture of Billy, Jesse and me taken in 1992 and the caption says, "Never leave your wing man." There is an old green Army jacket with the sleeves cut off and words that Billy wrote in with a marker that say, "Prospect Missouri." Also, wrapped around the collar of the Army jacket is a pink Harley bandana that I was wearing in that

1992 picture. I love this room sometimes and other times I hate this room. The almost six years of living with criminals made me into the man I am but also ruined the person I was. I sat there for minutes staring into those images and lost souls but was soon brought back to this world by my one year old and three year old who just realized dad was home. Three years ago I realized that after 10 years of marriage I was not going to save the world but maybe some children of my own could help save me from that obsession.

Jesse called and said they decided to pull the plug on Billy and he was gone. I went to work the next few days but my mind kept drifting back to those days some 18 years ago. I had regrets of not staying in touch with Billy and wondered if I was being the wingman that I claimed to be. I had stayed in touch with Jesse but it's hard to stay in touch with everyone when you move away. I told my wife that I would ride my Harley back to Missouri to see Billy off and she said that would be fine. My wife and I had just come back from our annual spring motorcycle ride where we usually do around 3500 miles in five days but I was ready to ride again. The ride to Missouri was about 900 miles from where I lived now.

The time on the bike gave me the chance to relive all the moments from years ago and thank Billy for his instructions on life. When I was 60 miles from the funeral home I pulled over and switched my helmet. In 1992, I was on a ride with the boys when my helmet was stolen and I bought a cheap new one at a dealership in Texas. I immediately scratched it up and said no one would want to steal it because it was nasty. I came out of a gas station and Billy had glued dimes on my helmet and said that I was a dime dropper. Since those days more stuff has been glued to that helmet and even though I seldom wear it, it only seemed appropriate that I wear it to see Billy off. I put in my Molly Hatchet CD and headed towards the funeral home. There were approximately 30 Harleys in the parking lot. As I rode past the bikes I did not recognize any them and I was getting some hard looks from the guys around them. I shut my bike off and could not help but feel like it was the first time in a new bar at a new undercover investigation.

Jesse yelled, "Kid." After 12 hours on my bike that hug from Jesse never felt so welcomed. As word spread of the Kid's arrival a few old familiar faces appeared and once again I was home.

Jesse took me into the funeral home where more familiar faces greeted me and I saw Billy's wife. I told her I was sorry and she said she was surprised that I had ridden that far. I said I would ride to hell and back for Billy. I walked up to the casket and removed a glued-on dime from my helmet and placed it on Billy's casket and a tear squeezed from my eye. Over the next few hours stories where exchanged from the days long ago and I soon learned that I was no longer "The Kid" in this group of men. There were so many faces that I did not know but they had heard stories about me. Billy had an eight-year-old daughter by his second marriage and she was there. I felt bad that I had never met her.

The funeral home closed so the boys moved the party to a local bar. I stayed for a little while but decided to head to my parents house and see my dad. I walked out of the bar and up the deserted street and could not help but recall this was the same town I started my career off 18 years ago. It was the same town where I met Billy, the same town where

I met Jesse. I fired up my bike and blasted down the two lane black top road to my parent's house. It had been a long time since I had ridden a bike down this road but I could close my eyes and knew every turn up ahead. As I snaked through the pines that line my parents gravel driveway I recalled all the times I would shut my bikes off and coast home so they would not hear me come in late. I walked in my parent's house and found my father sitting in his wheel chair waiting on me. He asked how my ride was and I said "good." My father has been crippled since his first round of cancer in 1996 but it is still hard to grasp that he is confined to a wheel chair. My mom was out of town so dad offered me a frozen pizza. We ate the pizza and sat there for hours talking.

The next morning I loaded up my bike and headed to the chapel. There were approximately 50 Harleys and tons of police cars and police officers at the chapel. Billy's Harley family sat on the right side of the chapel and Billy's real family sat on the left side of the chapel. I smiled inside and recalled the day that Billy married his second wife and how the chapel was split the same way. I recalled how the small town where she grew up was over run by some bikers who looked bad but were the police. I sat there with my pink bandana on and the green Army vest Billy made for me and cried. I tried not to cry but could not stop the tears. I regretted not staying in touch with Billy and wondered if he knew how much he meant to me. I sat in that chapel and once again questioned what kind of a wingman I had become. Although old friends surrounded me, I felt alone and cold.

The cemetery was packed with police officers and police officers who looked like criminals. Billy had served in the Navy so he was given a 21-gun salute. The crowd thinned out and just Jesse, my Lt., Billy's two sons and I remained. Billy's two sons sat at the casket saying goodbye to a dad they really did not know. I tried to explain to them that the job back then was not designed for a man with a family, I'm not sure they understood.

My Lt., who started me off, put his arm around me and showed me the gravesite where his father who died of cancer was laid to rest. He then showed me the gravesite where his sister was laid to rest. I've known the Lt. for over 18 years and even though we stay in touch I never felt the bond like I felt with Jesse and Billy, but I did then. At the end of the cemetery the Lt.'s son sat on his bike He is now a police officer like his father. I remember him when he was a little boy and now I have to look up to him.

Jesse asked me if I was coming to the meal and I said I needed to get some air. We walked over to a tree where I told Jesse that we all struggle with balance because for years we lived like criminals and somehow we are supposed to forget those times and be the person we were before we went under, but that does not happen. I told him I loved him and play it safe because I'm not ready to bury another wingman. The remaining few fired their bikes up and rode back into town. I put my dime helmet back in saddlebag and placed the Army vest and bandana next to it. I put on my good helmet and took one final look at Billy's casket as it was being lowered in the ground. I said goodbye to Billy.

My journey home was going to be a long one. I had started late but I needed that night air to clear my head. I rode late into the night and called my wife who begged me to stop and get a hotel room. I took her advice and checked into a room. I found a Waffle House next door and sat down for a meal. I sat with my back to the wall and recalled the many meals I had with the boys at a Waffle House. I knew by now they were in some bar giving Billy another send off, probably the first of many in his honor. At this particular moment I struggled with balance; I have a perfect wife, two great boys and a job that pays the bills, but those days of living under are still with me.

Something I have learned about my struggle with balance and my inability to admit I struggle. We are all taught how the world works and how we are to fit in it. Most of us are taught the same principles of right and wrong, telling the truth and how one should act in public but some do not follow those standards; we refer to them as criminals. Unfortunately, in order to catch criminals, some people have to act like criminals on the outside but their souls remain pure, untouched. At age 21 I made the choice to join that group of people who pretend to be criminals. I have learned that I had to fragment my personality to successfully complete the mission. I see now that I fragmented my personality for almost six years. There is a certain high that is achieved when you fragment your personality and gain the trust of those that you are after. I recall that zone where lies and truth all blend into one and I believe my own story. In that zone I am a dope-buying machine and bulletproof. I have not forgotten the mission at hand but it is easier to be with the criminals than my real family. It has taken me a long time to admit this and realize this. It's time for the truth.

After I ate, I returned to my room and, within minutes, fell asleep. I am up at dawn and the ride home is a good one because I'm between point A and point B and I can't do anything about either one.

As I roll into my driveway my boys and wife greet me. I lift up number one son and put him on the gas tank and he smiles. I walk into our home office and hang the green Army vest back up along with the pink bandana. I place the dime helmet up on a shelf and pray it is many moons before it makes a trip to Missouri.

It has been a long time since Billy's last ride but it seems like yesterday. Once again I sit in this swamp in search of balance. The last thing I want to be is a person who blames his problems on some situation in his life. I chose to live with criminals and would not change that part of my life. If not for people like Billy and Jesse I would have been a failure at it. I do wish I could have figured out long ago that my search for the "zone" is just that, a search; it's not to be found. All of us who lived with criminals cope in our own way. I push my body to the limits in exercise; the way I ride my motorcycle and the way I hunt, are all in search of the zone. There are times that the zone shows itself in the form of my wife becoming a mother, the peace and calmness of my boys sitting on my lap before bed, the sun seeking its way through the thick swamp air in search of my untouched soul and when the darkness of the road and the rumble of the bike are in tune with my heart beat as I travel from point A to point B. Those times I feel bulletproof and there are not two worlds but one where there are no lies to remember, no mission at hand, just a man trying to live his life. I remember the boy I was some 18 years ago but he has changed. I dislike crowds now and the perfect day is a day in the woods with no one but my wife and kids. My soul is still untouched but my heart has lived with the worst of society.

The sun has now found a spot on my leg and it's warm, very warm. I have not heard a sound from the hogs but that's ok it's not about them at this particular moment it's about a man trying to find the kid that is lost inside him.

Written in memory of Billy, a friend, a father, a brother, a husband, a wingman, a man who could bring a smile to anyone's face, a man who will only be forgotten if we let that happen.

Written by "The Kid"

- WLV -

Crisis Concepts and Precepts

Lesson 9
"Triggers"

Triggers

To *trigger* something means to activate, generate, start, prompt, initiate, or spark something into action or to cause a reaction. The story, "Billy's Last Ride," is filled with triggers that prompted numerous memories for the author (Josey). Those memories were happy, sad, poignant, funny, and confusing. They elicited many emotions, sentiments, and reactions for Josey including pride, fear, loneliness, regret, sadness, confusion, understanding, joy, courage, loyalty, and honor among others. Almost all human beings experience triggers in their lives. Some generate pleasant thoughts; others spawn distressing or painful memories and strong internal feedback.

The most powerful triggers of all are those that are linked with traumatic events in our past. Smells, sounds, tastes, visual stimuli, physical sensations, thoughts, circumstances, places, situations, people, and events can trigger old painful memories and all of the associated emotions. If the person is suffering from Post Traumatic Stress Disorder, the stimuli that reminds him of a traumatic event can initiate intrusive memories, distressing arousal, a drive to isolate oneself from others, and even a wide range of physical symptoms.

Recognition of one's triggers goes a long way to reducing their power. When people are aware of the triggers, they can do more to avoid them outright. They are less prone to distressing surprises. When the triggers cause a person to re-experience the traumatic event in thoughts, emotions, and in bodily sensations, it is easier to gain control by recognizing them as reminders of a past event not a current experience. The reactions to current triggers are simply bringing up shadows of past wounds, not realities of the present. Knowing one's triggers is part of developing the roadmap for recovery from traumatic events.

Managing Triggers

Keep in mind that stress arousal is all about survival. The triggers associated with a past traumatic event are only remnants of the actual traumatic event, but they can fool the brain into thinking the same threat is underway again. The memories and images of the past event are so powerful that they discourage the person from going any where near that type of traumatic event again. The human system then reacts with all its alarm systems and defense mechanisms to a lesser stimulus as if it were preparing to struggle against the original trauma. This condition is called arousal. It may cause:

- Difficulty falling or staying asleep
- Irritability, anger, rage
- Loss of concentration
- Hyper-vigilance
- Intensified startle response
- Feelings of anxiety and sometimes panic

- Distressing memories, images and thoughts
- Dreams and nightmares
- Physical distress such as upset stomach, tremors, sweating
- Mental replays of the original traumatic event
- Emotional numbness
- Difficulties feeling love and balance
- Avoidance of people, places, events, circumstances and conversations that remind them of the traumatic experience
- Self blame / guilt feelings / shame
- Depression / suicidal thoughts or actions
- Difficulties in relationships
- Deterioration in physical health
- Headaches, nausea, rashes, gastrointestinal problems
- Low self image
- Hopelessness
- Obsessive behaviors
- Mental confusion
- Physical exhaustion
- Excessive fatigue

Things that may help:

1. Symptom patterns lasting four weeks or more may indicate PTSD or some other condition resulting from exposure to a traumatic experience. If a head injury (including concussion) was associated with the psychologically traumatic event, it is possible that a Traumatic Brain Injury (TBI) may have occurred. Both PTSD and TBI can occur together. That condition makes the assessment more complex and treatment is even more a necessity.

2. If you have not done so already, seek out a professional evaluation of your particular reactions.

3. Therapy can help, if you select a therapist who is very familiar with traumatic stress and if that therapist selects the proper treatment.

4. Write in a journal to help you identify the triggers.

5. Deliberately talking about the triggers and the original traumatic experiences to people you trust.

6. Avoid alcohol and drug use because they don't help and often make things much worse.

7. Take action to cope. Do not leave your care totally up to others. It is your life. Do something about it.

8. Develop a positive mental attitude is extremely helpful. People have to believe that they can beat PTSD and other stress conditions.

9. Recovery means hard work and persistence over time.

10. Recovery means learning from the trauma experience.

11. Learn stress management.

12. Accept appropriate help.

13. Learn about PTSD and other conditions resulting from an exposure to trauma.

14. Healing means a reduction in symptoms and an increase in the skills to manage those symptoms.

15. Healing does not mean forgetting about the trauma. The memories remain. What is most important is learning from the experience of trauma and becoming better, not bitter.

Controlling Painful Memories, Visual Images and Thoughts

It is common and natural to have memories of a traumatic event. Memories of a trauma are not bad in themselves.

What is bad is excessively intense and prolonged memories plus other symptoms of the trauma. It may help you if you understand that dreams, nightmares, and visual images are just mental images. They cannot actually physically hurt you.

1. Talk to people you trust about the trauma memories and images.
2. Most traumatic thoughts, memories, and images recede with time. Get help if they do not lessen over time.
3. Anxiety and panic attacks are not physically dangerous unless a person is in poor health. A panic attack is equivalent to a good physical workout in terms of the energy expended.
4. You will be as you think. If you think you can handle something, most likely you will.
5. Avoid thinking in negative terms. (e.g. This is going to kill me.) Instead say, "This is bad, but I can handle it."
6. Slowing the breathing rate can reduce tension.
7. Calm yourself. Act as if you are calm and under control.
8. Rest for a few minutes. Most of these uncomfortable sensations will pass with time.
9. Begin your activities again when things improve.
10. Coping requires practice.
11. Keep your eyes open. Observe your location. Notice details around you.
12. The trauma happened sometime in the past. You are in the present now and the same threats are not present now.
13. Get up. Get some movement going. Wash you face and hands.

14. Get someone who knows what you have been through on the phone and talk to that person. Let him or her know what you are going through at the moment.

15. A replay of past traumatic events is quite common. Expect those replays.

16. Discuss the experience with a counselor or at least a trusted friend.

17. Get up from your sleeping position. Do something to get you oriented to your present location. When you are sleeping, your brain will not distinguish between a dream sequence and reality. It will cause you to react as if the danger was clear and present. Your reactions are generated by a dream or nightmare, not by a real danger.

18. Indulge in lite physical activity.

19. Talk to someone if that is possible.

20. Maintain regular bedtime schedules.

21. Do something with your time when you can't sleep. When you feel tired, try going back to sleep.

22. Don't use alcohol, nicotine, or caffeine as they interfere with sleep. Sleep deprivation threatens health.

23. Exercise earlier in the day, not before bedtime.

24. Don't bottle up you anger. Express it in appropriate ways.

25. Slow down your thinking. Focus on the main issues. Lay out some objectives and work toward them.

26. Write reminder notes if you need them to keep yourself organized.

27. Keep a diary or journal about your trauma symptoms and how you managed them.
28. Avoid trying to accomplish everything at once. Split up tasks into controllable segments.
29. Communicate with people you know and trust.
30. Seek professional help if you cannot make progress on your own.

There are many paths to recovery after traumatic stress. Some of the pathways have proven to be highly effective. There is no shame in seeking assistance. The only shame is in choosing to do nothing when the opportunities are present. Try something!

Chapter 10

Santa Claus, Easter Bunny, and the Tooth Fairy

I can recall the morning like it was yesterday. I came down the steps and the floor beneath our Christmas tree was loaded with presents. I turned and saw boot prints from our fireplace to the Christmas tree. Santa Claus had come. Hours later after the wrapping paper had been torn from our presents I found myself in my dad's closet examining his work boots; they were covered in ashes from our fireplace. There was no Santa, why did my parents tell me there was.

When my wife and I decided to have kids I told her the above story and we contemplated being honest with our children but we decided to follow in the footsteps of those before us.

Four years ago I found myself with a full-grown man sitting in front of me with tears in his eyes. The man, a firefighter, had tried to save the life of a small boy by breathing his air into the boy's lungs. The little boy lived for a day and died. The full-grown man showed me a picture of his own son. Both boys were the same age.

I called my wife and told her I felt like the times our children wake up with an ear ache and all we can do is hold them and assure them it will get better but in reality it is the medicine that will make them feel better. I told my wife I finally get the Santa Claus, Easter Bunny, and the Tooth Fairy approach to our children. As we grow we will soon learn of the ugliness that life can send our way and there will be days we will need to believe in something we cannot see but we can feel it in our heart.

A child seldom asks how it is possible an overweight guy can fit down a chimney, or why an Easter Bunny leaves eggs in our yards, or why a Tooth Fairy would want our old teeth. Children are just glad that someone or something cares about them that particular day. A child seldom questions anything about the "why," a child just believes.

I told my wife how important it is as adults that we not question why this person was killed and why I survived this horrible event. What is important is that we believe in something we cannot see, we dig deep in our heart and soul and remember coming down the steps at Christmas, running through the yard to get those eggs, and checking under our pillow. We remember the magic of it all and that someone cares about us that day, the very day our world stopped and tragedy struck our hearts.

We need to believe that it will get better; we need to know that the pain in our hearts will never go away, but it will not hurt as bad. We need to believe in something we cannot see, cannot touch, cannot taste, cannot hear, and cannot smell. I think that something is called *faith* but to a child it's an overweight man in a red suit, a rabbit that likes chicken eggs, and a small person with wings. We need faith that the next day will be better and this horrible event will not destroy us but defines, instead, who we become, a group of people who survived to believe in another day.

I often wish when I have that someone sitting in front of me with much more than an childhood ear ache I could wave a magic stick, I could slide down a chimney, I could hide eggs in their yard and make all the pain go away, but I can't. All I can do is try and find the child in them that is buried under all that pain and hope they have the faith to believe it will get better.

- WLV -

Crisis Concepts and Precepts

Lesson 10
"Positive Outcome Expectancy"

Note:

Our parents and grandparents knew that children need excitement, expectations, imagination, magic, and hope to develop healthy, flexible, and adaptable minds. Children especially need belief and trust in the important adults in their lives, particularly their parents. The combination of realistic beliefs in reliable and trustworthy adults and enriched mental stimulation by means of play and imagination develops healthy children and dependable adults. That being said, Josey and his wife appear to have made the right decision in regard to their children on the issue of imagination.

Sometimes people can inspire us and give us the courage and the motivation to keep going against the odds. Sometimes we can be the inspiration for others. To deal with a crisis and recover from a traumatic experience we must believe that things can get better and that we might make a difference for ourselves and for others. Believing is a powerful, driving force. Coupling that force with specialized training and guiding principles can have extraordinary influence on the reduction of pain and distress when dealing with a crisis. All of the seven Crisis

Intervention principles have enormous value. But, as the paragraphs below indicate, one stands out from the other six as a principle with special significance.

In Lesson 2 we covered the seven principles of crisis intervention. They are repeated here for the sake of convenience:

1. **Simplicity**
2. **Brevity**
3. **Innovation**
4. **Pragmatism**
5. **Proximity**
6. **Immediacy**
7. **Expectancy**

When psychologists explored these seven principles to see if one or two were more helpful than the others to people in a state of crisis, one stood out as clearly more important than all of the others. It was an expectancy of a positive outcome. In other words - **Hope.** People could tolerate extreme difficulties and deprivations if there was hope that they could overcome adversity and that things could eventually get better.

It is very important not to brush aside an individual's or a group's traumatic experience. The approach, instead, should be: "I know that this situation was very difficult and painful for you. My experience tells me that most people will recover from this tragedy. That's what I would expect for each of you. Until you can find your own path to recovery, I will do whatever I can to assist you."

The story in Chapter 10 is a story of hope and faith and a belief in a power beyond us. It starts off with a distressed and emotionally rattled firefighter sitting with a peer support person. The firefighter is crying because a child has died despite his efforts to restore the child's breathing. The presence of the peer can be reassuring because it figuratively states that the peer is there to help until the person finds a way out of this depressing situation. The peer presence carries another, although implied, message that although things are painful now there is a positive outcome expectation that the next day will be better for the firefighter than the one he is currently in. This story that says life is still worth living even after a tragedy because someone cares enough about the firefighter to show-up and offer emotional support, consolation and a helping hand. People respond positively when they realize that there are others who are willing to leave their homes and travel to be there where people are in need and adversity has struck. Pitching in, sharing the load, listening, encouraging, supporting and caring are all part of building positive outcome expectancy. With that, people can get up and care for themselves and recover. Then they can go back to their jobs and try to make a difference for another person.

Chapter 11

My Full Moon

Dad reached across the creek and grabbed my hand to steady me as I crossed. The moon was very full but I still had trouble seeing the dry rocks to put my little feet on them. My right foot slipped off a rock and my foot got wet. Dad pulled me forward and said it will be ok. My wet foot soon did not matter as I heard the sound of the coonhound barking up in the hollow. I followed my dad as he followed our neighbor to see if the hound had actually treed a coon. Once again, the hound did not tree a coon that we could see but I was with my dad and felt like a man.

A long time after that night, I floated there on top of the water and starred deep into the full moon. I thought back to that hollow with my dad and how I wished I were there instead of here. Occasionally the music from the boat and the voices of the people on the boat would drift between the full moon and me. The voices had no idea I was a police officer sent here to gain their trust and live in their world. Once their trust was gained, I would buy whatever it was they were selling and many months later they would find out that I was not their friend, but in their eyes, the enemy. Before long the voices became louder and the name I was using at the time was said repeatedly. I swam to the boat leaving behind my full moon and the hollow that I was in with my dad.

There would be many more times over the next six years that I would escape the world I was living in by looking at the full moon and drifting back to that hollow with my dad. One night in particular I tried to drift back to that hollow but the memory was not as clear. All I could think about was all the other full moons since that night and soon I could not recall that night at all.

Over the next ten years I would wear many hats as I followed my calling to be a peacekeeper, and the innocence of my youth slowly but surely disappeared. I soon figured out that the ugly side of being an adult soon replaced thoughts, smells, and visual images that were special to me. I truly love being married to my wife and being a father to my two boys but, as I follow my calling, I see many things that I wish I could forget.

I traveled by plane to a place far from the tangled waters of my beloved swamp to wear my new hat and talk to some ordinary men who did their best on a very tragic day. As I sat with each one of them and they peeled away their layers of armor and insulation, their visual images unfolded in front of me. The smells they smelled, the flesh they touched, and the efforts to keep life inside a body became things I too wanted to forget. I struggled with my urge to try and make them feel better when I knew that was not my job. My job was to redirect, to clarify, to help them understand that their reactions were normal, to focus their thinking, and restore faith that one day the memories of this tragic day would pass. No one can make a person feel better about a tragic day but him or her self and my job was to direct these folks to that day when they would be better.

After several days of wearing that hat, I took a plane back home to see my wife and boys and find a place to put the layers of tragedy that I did not check on the plane but carried onto the plane. A friend who manages a large farm asked for help in removing the wild hogs that were costing him thousands of dollars in crop damage. I was only home a few hours when I found myself driving to his farm wearing a different hat, my hunting hat. We started at ten o'clock at night and hunted by the full moon using night vision scopes on our rifles.

I looked at the moon several times and had no luck recalling those visual images of that night with my dad in that hollow. Dad died a few months later and when I saw an old kerosene lantern at my parent's house I could finally recall that night in the hollow. I could still smell the kerosene burning from that long-ago night and recall my dad's callused hand helping me across the creek.

We encountered a large group of hogs in the field and killed several. We were loading them in the truck when I felt a pain in my groin area. I never told my friend and we continued to hunt through the night. At daylight I drove home and cleaned the hogs and put them in my smoker. When I lay down to go to sleep I had been up for 40 hours and everything that I carried on the plane seemed to be gone but I still had a pain in my groin. A few days later I went to a doctor and it was determined I had a double hernia.

I laid there in pre-op not looking forward to this operation, but I needed to have this hernia fixed. The nurse explained to me that I needed to wear these compression socks. I knew what they were since my dad wore them for years after his second cancer surgery. As she slid the socks over my legs I felt very much like my dad and had no trouble recalling that the lack of circulation in my dad's lower legs caused them to rot and, ultimately, it is what killed him. I can still smell the rotten flesh today, everyday. I could not wait for the gasman to come and put me to sleep as my heart raced towards my legs.

The next few weeks were painful but I kept the compression socks on and soon they became just socks, not a constant reminder of my dad's death. I found myself back on the farm hunting the hogs by the full moon. I was restricted from lifting but was able to wear my hunting hat with no problem. The incisions in my groin healed and soon I was able to lift again with no problem. The hog hunts continued every month and would end with me being awake for 40 hours. After one hog hunt I was taking out my dog for his last bathroom break and stood there mentally and physically exhausted wishing he would hurry up. I looked up at the full moon and recalled the night before as we hunted the hogs and never thought once about all the other ugly full moons I have tried so hard to forget over the some eighteen years of wearing many hats.

Once again I found myself on that plane traveling to a place far from my beloved swamp to talk to those men who were preparing for the one year anniversary of the tragic day they were thrown into. As we reflected on that day and noted their progress I told one man of my ability or should I say faith to recapture my full moon. I explained that we need faith that the tarnished, damaged, flawed, and stripping of innocence will come back to everything around us but we must believe.

I boarded that plane and what I carried on was not as heavy as last time. I once again found myself on the farm hunting hogs by the full moon. I once again found myself lying down after being up for 40 hours and my wife tucking me in like I was one of her babies. I told her to put wood on the smoker in four hours and make sure the temperature stays at 200 degrees. My wife said "Is it worth it?" I asked "Is what worth it?" My wife said, "What you do to your body to hunt hogs, the being up for 40 hours." I proceeded to tell my wife the full moon story and I said, "It is worth every minute." I said, "After 18 years I have my moon back and I will clutch it in my hands, my heart, and my soul like our little one does when he wraps his 'blankie' around his hands at night when he sleeps." I told her so many things are taken from me as I follow this path and wear the hats that are presented to me. My innocence is stripped from me as I make this choice to stop others from being tarnished by the evilness of man and sometimes the way life comes at us but I must have faith that some of that innocence will return or be replaced by a fresher memory. My wife said "Okay" and kissed me on the forehead like one of her young 'uns.

As my mind and body came to rest, I thought about those ordinary men who did their best on a tragic day that no one could be prepared for. I could not see the full moon from my bed but I could feel her shining down. I look forward to the next hog hunt or the next plane ride to that place where tragedy has struck and lost souls await a full moon to guide them home.

– WLV –

Crisis Concepts and Precepts

Lesson 11
"Colliding Worlds"

The Collision of Worlds

When our experiences on the job remind us of someone or something close to home our separate worlds of work and our private life at home collide. All it takes is a child who has been critically wounded or killed. If the child is about the same size as our own child or if he looks even a little like our own child, our worlds are colliding. It doesn't have to be a child case to make our worlds collide. If an adult looks like your mother or father or a brother or sister or even a good friend, you can get the collision of worlds.

There may also be collisions of our past worlds with our present worlds. Josey starts off having vivid past memories of a special time hunting with his Dad by the light of a full moon. For years he could recall that image until he was stressed by his undercover work. Then the image was lost to him when his undercover full moon experiences collided with his past. He believed he would get that special memory of the full moon with his Dad, and indeed he did. But, the full moon image only returned when he was no longer doing undercover work and only when stimulated by the powerful impact of his Dad's death.

The peer support work Josey was doing to help people through tragedies in their community was, and still is, of great importance to him. As difficult and as painful as it is, his peer support work gives him great personal satisfaction. Being far happier than when he was an undercover agent, helps him to keep the image of that special night with his Dad hunting under a beautiful full moon. He feels he is helping others to find their own full moon to guide them to a place of peace and safety.

Worlds colliding can be caused by any stimulus. Seeing the kerosene lantern and smelling its fuel burn brought back vivid memories for Josey including the full moon he missed so much. It could be a smell, a taste, a visual image, a body sensation, a sound, an article of clothing, compression stockings or an object. When Josey had to undergo surgery the compression stocking he was required to wear distressed him because his Dad had to wear them for several years before he died. Situations, circumstances, events, experiences, emotions of the present can easily draw on the power of the past. A combination of events can be more powerful than any single event. The private and professional worlds collide also when something we encounter on the job reminds us of our own childhood or teen years.

Here is a personal example. I was driving home from work when I was about 24 years old. I was listening to the radio and singing along with a song and feeling happy and content. I saw two boys dueling with sticks on someone's front lawn. Suddenly, I jammed on my breaks, jumped out of my car and started screaming at the boys to stop. They dropped their sticks and ran away. I picked up the two sticks and broke them into toothpick sized sticks and then threw them into a trashcan with considerable force. I got back in my car and drove about 100 feet. I pulled off to the side of the road. I was shaking. Suddenly 17 year-old images started flooding into my mind. I was stunned to be thinking of something that happened so many years before especially since I had not thought of it in all that time. Two different worlds had suddenly collided and my happy and content feelings were replaced by something dark and ominous. I was now tense, fearful, full of dread. I was feeling nauseous, light headed, and weak. What was going on? Why such an impact?

My current world had inadvertently collided with my childhood world because of the behaviors of some young boys on someone's lawn. Knowing what caused one of our worlds to collide with another one of our worlds is not automatic. Sometimes we do not know what caused the collision. It may remain a mystery to us. When we can figure it out, however, we experience relief, understanding, even peace. Knowing what happened lessens the chance we will be surprised and shocked again. Understanding gives us power.

As I sat there shaking, however, my two worlds' collision became clear. When I was 7 years old and in a day camp I was participating in a field day at a local park. I was sitting on a picnic table waiting for lunch with my group. Two boys in my group began to duel with sticks. Then things turned really horrible. I saw a stick penetrate an eye of one of the boys. I was terrified and extremely distressed. I felt sick to my stomach. I felt weak kneed, lightheaded and nauseous. The same feelings and reactions of my childhood came right back as if I were 7 years old and sitting on a park table watching two kids duel. My worlds had collided.

Sometimes we may have to help a person come to an understanding of which of their worlds collided and why those reactions are normal, although painful. Usually when a person grasps the meaning behind their current reaction, they calm down and their emotions and thoughts and bodily manifestations of distress become more manageable.

The collision of worlds is common and it is **not** a sign of weakness, instability or mental problems. The collision of worlds can cause disruption in performance and heightened emotional and physical arousal until a person figures out why that particular stimulus has generated so much distress. Understanding brings about recovery fairly quickly.

Chapter 12

Stephen and the Three Wooden Crosses

I walked into Stephen's parent's bedroom and told them that Dan and I wanted Stephen to come over to my house and camp out. Stephen's mom said, "You promise that you will not go to town?" I said yes. Stephen's mom said, "Ok, just bring him back in the morning." Stephen had made some bad grades in school so his parents grounded him and took the keys to his four-wheel drive truck. We piled in Dan's truck and drove down the two-lane asphalt road that snaked between two ridges. We turned off the asphalt road and drove down the gravel road that separated the two farms. Dan lived with his parents on one farm and I lived with my folks on the other. We camped out that night on a ridge and dreamed of where our lives would take us. The next morning Stephen's dad called our parent's homes and said he needed to come home. There had been an accident. A week later I found myself riding my motorcycle across another state while Stephen's mom was being laid to rest in a small cemetery off that same asphalt road that led to our houses. Stephen's mom was special to me and she trusted me, but I could not be there that day for him.

A few weeks later Stephen had to replace the ignition switch in his truck because he could never find where his mom had hidden his keys. Stephen and I were in his truck climbing some steep hills on an electric power line on a cold afternoon when the song 'Stairway to heaven" came on the radio. He looked at me and said it was a good day to climb that stairway. Stephen was always a risk taker but the last few weeks he was more risky than ever. In the months that followed her death I found myself sliding down gravel roads, climbing steep power lines, and watching the other keys in his truck ignition switch rocking back and forth. Many times I was scared, but those rocking keys seemed to calm me as Stephen searched for that stairway.

Many years later I received a call for a peer support assignment. I thought hard about Stephen as I made the seven-hour drive to see a man who had lost three family members in an accident that happened on a power line. I had seen Stephen a few times in the last 25 years and knew he was married and had kids, but we never spoke about his mom and that horrible day when she died. I never told him I was sorry for not being there at the funeral. All I did after she died was hang on inside his truck as he tried to climb that stairway and never acted like I was scared.

I entered the room and found a man and his wife who both looked like they had not slept in days. The man had a cell phone in front of him and a watch that was also a phone; I named him the Programmer in my head. His wife immediately looked to me for answers to questions that had not even been asked yet. Over the next three hours they told me their story. They were near an electric power line, having a family gathering, when there was an accident. The whole family witnessed the crash. The Programmer ran up to the crash site and found his son, mother, and aunt dead. The Programmer's brother was alive, but with severe injuries. The Programmer used his training to render medical treatment and his brother was now in critical condition. The Programmer told me with tears in his eyes, "no one should have to triage his family." I sat there and felt like I was back in that truck with Stephen. I could not let them see that their story scared me. I dug deep inside myself and went beyond the training that I had to guide people to a brighter day, and spoke from my heart because it was all I could find. My drive home was long and many times I cried because, as a parent, this was the worst story I had ever heard. I normally try to feel the pain of those that I support, but not in this case. I did not want to feel the pain; just being in the room with them was painful enough.

Over the next weeks and months I soon learned that in this case I named him correctly, he would text much more than talk. I would struggle for the right words to type into my phone and pray that what I typed would help him though this moment. After several months, I realized the Programmer and his family were above my pay grade and I needed to refer them to someone who really does support and treatment for a living. I volunteer at a non-profit that caters to military, police, and fire personnel. I convinced the Programmer that he should bring his family there and receive treatment. After an 18-hour drive, the Programmer got out of his car with his family following close behind. Over the next week, people were brought in to work with the Programmer, his wife and kids at no charge. Once again, there was no need to try to feel the pain; it was in the air we were breathing. We did share some laughs and smiles, and for a brief moment or two, that power line was a lot farther away than 18 hours.

The non-profit place seemed to help the Programmer, but even in normal life, it peaks and valleys, and for this family their valleys were very deep. I struggled and tried to be what the Programmer needed, but many times I felt like I was back in the truck with Stephen on that power line, many miles from the Programmers power line. After about six months from the crash, I asked the Programmer if he would like to return to the crash site, and he said yes. I had asked many times before and he had said no. The Programmer told me that once his brother found out we were going back to the crash site that he also wanted to go. I contacted some of the key emergency responders that were there that day and asked them to buy some wooden crosses and surprise the Programmer and his family with them as they drove to the crash site. The Programmer, his wife, his brother, and his brother's wife met me in a parking lot not far from the power line. The Programmer's brother was still suffering from injuries, but was alive. I followed the Programmer to the crash site and on the side of the road there was a small group of men and women with their hats off in respect. The Programmer drove right past them and never stopped. I called him and said they have something for you. We parked in the power line and watched the group of uniformed men and women walk toward us; it looked like a parade of heroes. They presented the Programmer and his family with the wooden crosses. The Programmer wrapped his arms around his cross like a father wraps his arms around his child. The Programmer's brother had made three wooden white crosses and asked if they could take the ones we gave them home and they would use theirs at the crash site and I said sure. I named the Programmers brother the Cabinet Maker in my head just by the way he was looking around and trying to put the pieces together.

The Programmer, his wife, the Cabinet Maker, his wife and I began the long walk to the crash site. They talked and recalled what each one remembered about that day. I listened, but once again I was back in that truck with Stephen on a power line with hills, but, this one was flat. I could hear the song in my head, I could feel the bounce of his truck, and that look in his eyes, and the same look I could see in the eyes of all four people. Most of all, I could once again breathe the pain that was in the air. It felt good to walk that long road. We reached the crash site and there was still some crash debris there. As the Cabinet Maker tried to put the pieces together all I could do was stand back and watch. They all gathered around the debris and said a prayer. They placed the three homemade crosses at the debris and I will forever recall the Cabinet Maker as he used a hammer to drive the crosses into the ground despite his injuries. Many times, while I stood there, the Programmer looked over at me as I tried to blend in with the trees and he thanked me for being there. I know many times I tell my boy's, accidents happen and it's not your fault. It seems to work for them, but when it comes to adults it really never seems to work. For some reason, when we become adults, we feel we can control everything around us. I kept my distance from the Cabinet Maker because I had no idea what to say to him, but I never really knew what to say to the Programmer over the last six months. The walk back to our cars was not as long as the walk to the crash site. At our cars, a few of the emergency personnel, who are also a part of the Programmer's brotherhood, were waiting on us. Hugs and thanks were given and for the first time since I met the Programmer he seemed at peace.

It's been months since that day and I find myself once again trying to process the events that are handed to us. I struggle with the crosses that some of us have to bear, why some of them have to be so heavy. No amount of training could have ever prepared me for the Programmer and the crosses he has to bear, but he has taught me much. I have told him more than once, this is his journey and he corrects me and says, "It's our journey." Many years after Stephens's mom died I found myself kneeling down next to her gravesite by the light of the moon as it shone down between the two ridges off that asphalt road. I said my peace to her and explained why I was not there that day. I hope she understood that sometimes we run when we are scared. A few years ago when Stephen walked through the VFW door to pay respects for my father who just died, I once again was back on that power line. I thought hard as he stood in front of me and said he was sorry my dad had died. As he walked away once again I was too scared to tell him I was sorry his mom died and I was not there that day.

I never said my peace to Stephen, but now I see that what I did back then for him is not much different than what I do now. I ride up a power line or walk down a power line, but I stand by a man as he bears his crosses, and on certain days I may help him carry those crosses. I may not always know what to say, but I have learned the importance that the power lines that Stephen and the Programmer climb, they never climb alone. The journey with the Programmer has taught me that once your walk through that door and hear their story you must be committed to make that climb or in his case that walk.

Our society seems to accept our physical wounds easier than the emotional wounds. We know how to help blind persons find their way, but with emotional wounds we cannot see what needs to be treated. As a society we look to people like me to heal those torn with emotional wounds, but in reality, all people, like the Programmer, need is to be treated the same way they were treated before the event that left them torn. The Programmer, and those like him, just wants people to never forget those that climb the stairway before us, even when it was just an accident.

It's almost daylight and the ground some 20 feet under me is becoming clearer. You can find me up here or on the ground, but the woods is where I go to heal my superficial wounds from the work I do. I've had many ask me over the years how can I subject myself time and time again to the adult nightmares of others and for me it is easy. I've spent the last 25 years doing what I can to make the world a safer place, but when we can help one of our own get back on the truck, back in the car, or just sleep at night, the reward cannot be described. It's hard the first time you walk through the door and hear their story, it's hard when they call wanting answers that no one has, and it's hard when you watch them bury their own. But, if you commit to the journey, you will make an influence on their life that will matter to them and everyone around them. The sun is up now and on a flat power line the grass is growing and the trees have healed themselves from the crash. As the sun breaks through the trees and shines down on a two-lane asphalt road, the sound of sirens can be heard bouncing off the trees. The Programmer reaches up and lowers his truck's visor so he can see the road ahead. The Programmer is back doing what he does best; helping others.

-WLV-

Crisis Concepts and Precepts

Lesson 12
"Follow Through and Follow-up"

Note: As Josey points out in his story, the fact that a peer support person is well trained and experienced does not mean that he or she will always know what to say when faced with someone's tragedy. Sometimes the pain in those we attempt to help is overwhelming and it stuns us. It can be difficult to wrap our brains around their shock, confusion, and loss. There is no perfect set of words to make everything better. In the end it is not what we say that will matter most. What counts is how well we listen. The most important element of all is being present in some particularly low point in someone's life and being willing to do simple things that let the person know we care. Our best suggestion on being a good peer is to follow your heart and let it guide you in what you do and say to support a pained and troubled person. Sometimes, just showing up and standing by can count more than we can imagine.

Follow Through

Follow through means completing the mission, getting the job done. In crisis intervention and peer support, the interventionist must make sure that the intervention is complete. Completeness can be judged by one of several conditions:

1) The person you are assisting gains emotional control and is capable of making his or her own crisis action plan. Your support can be reduced or removed all together.

2) Assistance is provided through all the steps or stages of crisis intervention. You complete everything you can do for the person or for a group of people under the circumstances and it is time to disengage, at least temporarily.

3) The person receiving assistance decides to stop you from doing anything additional. The crisis support personnel never force anyone to accept assistance if they choose to reject help.

Strategic Planning

Proper planning enhances the potential that the crisis intervention will be complete. It is essential that we avoid rapid fire, knee jerk reactions to what is probably a more complex problem than it appears at first view. We need to slow down a little, listen carefully, breathe, think and then develop an effective crisis action plan. There is a strategic planning formula to guide through the development of a crisis action plan. The 5-part formula for strategic planning is:

Target(s): Who needs assistance? Who does not need assistance?

Types: What types of assistance are most likely to be helpful?

Timing: When will the interventions be likely to have the best effects?

Theme: What are the issues concerns, questions, problems, threats and considerations that may influence any part of the plan?

Team: Who is being deployed to provide the support? Are the personnel the best match for the needs of those requiring assistance?

Follow-up

Unlike some household cleaning products, crisis intervention is not a "once-and-done" approach. Follow-up is a critical and necessary part of crisis work. Crisis states can be tenacious. No one should assume that a person is fully recovered just because they sounded or looked better after the first contact with them. It takes time to process the event and understand what has happened and the meaning the experience has for the person or the people involved. A person seen on Monday evening may appear to have been doing reasonably well. But that does not mean that they will be doing well Tuesday evening or Wednesday morning.

Informal Follow-up

There are numerous ways to follow-up with a person suffering through the aftereffects of a crisis. Informal or casual follow-up techniques include:

- Telephone calls to check on the person's welfare
- Texts messaging
- Emails
- Workplace visits
- Off-site individual support
- Home visits (as long as the person does not object)
- Informational, educational meetings

- Social gatherings (be present, but don't try to get discussions on the critical incident or the crisis reaction going)

Direct contact with the person in crisis is the most desirable approach. Seeking information from a colleague or from a supervisor should be among the last methods to learn about the crisis reactions and needs of a person in distress. The most frequent informal follow-up is an individual conversation. Assist, whenever possible, with the fulfillment of appropriate requests. For example, if a person wishes to return to the scene and view the location of a tragedy, a peer support person might accompany that person. It is very hard to return to a place of traumatic stress by oneself. There are many disturbing emotional reactions that could get stirred up. Company helps to reduce distress.

Formal Follow-up

Formal follow up services include:

- Critical Incident Stress Debriefing (CISD)
- Referrals for medical care
- Referrals for psychotherapy
- Brief Crisis-Oriented Therapy
- A session or two of Eye Movement Desensitization and Reprocessing
- Educational / informational classroom sessions
- Progressive desensitization

Most follow-ups are completed in two to five contacts unless therapy is required. Then the therapist will work with the client to establish a therapy schedule for as long as necessary. Peers rarely have to deal with lengthy follow-ups. Sometimes, in unusual circumstances, peers will need to check in with traumatized people periodically for six months to a year. There are a few cases in which a peer has been involved in follow–up beyond a year. They should only do that sort of follow-up support with a mental health professionals providing consultation.

Chapter 13

Pearl Pond

My mother knelt down in front of me and laced up my funny looking shoes. I said, "But momma, I just want to wear cowboy boots. She said, "These shoes will help your feet grow right." I said, "Momma, is there something wrong with me?" Momma said, "No baby, you are just different, but special to me."

I thought of that day as I drove down along this field to talk to a man about hunting on his farm. A guy had told me about this man who owned a large farm and lived back in the woods. He said the man had retired from law enforcement and was *different*, but that he might let me hunt on his farm. The house I pulled up to was modest and hidden back in the woods. I knocked on the door and before my hand was by my side the door was snatched open. A tall, thin man stood before me and said, "What do you want?" I asked, "Are you, Mr. Rob?" The man said, "Yes, what do you want?" I said, "I called you on the phone about hunting on your farm." He said, "Oh yeah, come on, get in the truck." We got into a small pickup truck that was old and worn. At first, he did not say much so I just sat there trying to figure out how to break the ice with this man. His big hands were wrapped around the steering wheel, but they were very thin, his skin just seemed to be hanging on. As we drove around the farm he asked me who I worked for and I told him. He said, "I heard a guy moved in down the road and that he worked for the same outfit I did back in the day." He said, "I was a pilot for you all back in the day, but I don't fly anymore." When he said that, he looked at me, and for a brief moment he smiled.

The farm was very big, had open fields, and lots of planted pine trees. He told me that we could not go down some of the logging roads because the limbs were growing across the road. He said, "I pay a young boy to keep them trimmed back, but all he wants to do is ride around on the tractor." I told him I'd be glad to keep the roads trimmed, that it was one of my jobs while growing up on our small farm. He said that would be fine. When the farm tour was over he parked the truck and said, "That was your five cent tour, good luck." He got out of the truck and as he walked back to the house I asked, "Mr. Rob, can I hunt tonight?" "Sure," he answered, not looking back.

I grabbed my rifle and walked the logging roads that night. I saw a deer at the edge of the field, shot it and loaded it into the basket on the back of my Jeep. I drove up to Mr. Rob's house and knocked on the door. Once again he snatched the door open. He looked at me and asked what I needed. I said, "I killed a deer back there in the big field, you want to see it?" He said, "You do not have to show me the deer you kill and closed the door." As I drove away from his house I thought maybe everyone in this small farming community was right about this man, he was different, but most of my life people have said I was different.

The farm was not far from my house and soon became my home away from home. I explored the planted pines and found the place that became my heaven on earth, the swamp. A creek runs through the swamp and most of the year there is water in the creek. One evening, I attempted to cross the creek during flood conditions and I found myself being sucked under the water. If not for the training I had received from the Marine Corps boot camp on swimming in full gear I think this story would have had a different ending. I would imagine for most folks that the swamp is not a pretty place, but to me it had very little signs that humans had ever been there. The mosquitoes looked like small planes and in the summer months the swamp air was so thick it felt hard to breath. There were cottonmouth snakes around every water hole and wild hogs tucked back in the brushy spots. I liked that I could make a foot print in the mud and a week later it was the only footprint still there.

As we gradually became friends, 'Mr. Rob' eventually became just plain Rob to me. I would see Rob in the afternoons, riding in his diesel truck that he was so proud of, around the farm. There were four ponds on the farm, but Rob would go to one particular pond every evening. That pond was called the Pearl pond. One evening, I saw Rob near Pearl Pond. I watched from a distance through binoculars and saw that Rob just sat in his truck looking at the pond. I decided from that point forward that I would just stay clear of the Pearl pond because to Rob it was his favorite place on the farm.

Over the next few years the ice between Rob and me thawed and we talked more and more. He would talk about his time in the Army during the Vietnam War and flying planes for "my outfit," as he called it. He told me he never married and had no children, that when his dad died he retired early and came home to run the family farm, that he had no plans of coming back home, but the road had changed in front of him and he had to do what was right.

My role on the farm went from the guy that hunted, to the guy who fixed things, kept the logging roads cleared, managed the wild hogs and deer from doing crop damage, to security. My wife would make plates of food for Rob. I would leave the food on his front porch rail in the early morning hours as I headed back to hunt or just go to the swamp. It did not take long for Rob to realize that the swamp was my heaven on earth and then would make jokes that I was headed to the swamp to get some swamp yoga.

One evening, Rob called me on the phone. He sounded sad. He talked about some of the things he had done and seen especially in the army, and how it bothered him. I just listened. I had learned early on that in order to be Rob's friend, he dictated what he wanted. If he wanted to talk I would listen. If he wanted me to talk he would ask a question. If he wanted to be left alone he would not answer the door when I knocked and would merely drive by me on the farm. I knew things bothered him, but I never pushed or pried. I just made sure he always knew I was there for him. After that evening, Rob opened up more about the things he was trying to forget. I told him some of my stories and things I had done which was just one more thing we had in common.

Rob was an avid shooter, but as his health declined it was difficult for him to shoot at our target range. I decided to build him a range that he could shoot at from his truck at the Pearl pond. I heard his diesel start up that evening as he headed down to the Pearl pond and a few minutes later I heard him shooting. When he came up the hill from the pond I was sitting in my Jeep and that day was a day he wanted to talk. He thanked me for the shooting range and once again he talked about those things that bothered him.

Rob was the first person I told that my wife was pregnant. I asked if he would mind if my wife and I could walk the logging roads together so that she could stay in shape. Rob congratulated me and said, "Walk all you want." We walked every evening and even touched the edge of the swamp a few times. On those walks, we came up with name for our new baby. I went down into the swamp before the baby was born and went to what I call the "special place." I crossed the creek by using a tree that had fallen over it and removed an empty gallon milk jug from my backpack. I kneeled down to fill the jug with swamp water when out of the corner of my eye I saw the white mouth of a cottonmouth. The swamp has a way of constantly reminding me that I am nothing more than a visitor. I took the swamp water, boiled it and drove 900 miles with my wife, and our new baby boy. We travelled so that the priest who married us could baptize our baby. Our priest was a Marine who had served in the Vietnam War, and he too has been called "different." My parents were in the church that day as was my friend Rob, who had left the Pearl pond long enough to drive that diesel truck to see the swamp water baptize our son. We gave Rob a mason jar full of holy swamp water that day.

My son became a welcomed addition to the farm life. I bought a backpack that held him and we went everywhere on the farm together. Soon my wife was pregnant with our next child and once again we walked the logging roads together and came up with a name for our new baby. Our son also went on these walks and enjoyed the view from his backpack. Our second son was baptized in the same church with the same holy swamp water, but Rob's health had further declined so he did not make the trip.

My boys were learning about farm life and being in the woods, which is how I was raised. When my oldest son killed his first deer on the farm he asked if we could take it by and show Uncle Rob. I said, "No we will just give him a picture." I gave the picture to Rob and he said, "Thanks." He told me that he was sitting on the front porch one day and that a preacher man came to visit him. The preacher said, "You need to come to my church, Mr. Rob." Rob told me that he proceeded to tell the preacher man some of the things that he had done and seen. Rob said the preacher man heard his story and then he just left. Rob asked me if I would put a gate up at the end of his driveway and I did.

Recently, my boys and I parked at Rob's house and walked down into the woods to hunt. We had only been there about 30 minutes when a deer stepped out and my oldest son shot it. We walked down to the deer and my oldest son said, "Daddy this will be some good meat for our family." I asked the boys if they wanted to walk back to the Jeep with me or stay with the deer. They both said they wanted to stay with the deer. I followed the little road out and came to the road that led to the Pearl pond. I looked down at the pond and could still see the water even though the sun had set. I looked up the hill to Rob's house and the light next to his easy chair was not on. I moved over a little to get a better look and I still could not see the light through the window. Rob always left that light on. As I walked up the road I did not see his diesel truck parked in the carport. Then it hit me, like it always does, that Rob has been dead for over three years. I always say, "Damn you, Rob."

In the woods, I could hear my boys making more noise than a group of young raccoon hound pups. I walked up the hill with tears in my eyes. I passed by his front porch and recalled the day that my dad died. My mom had called to tell me that dad died and I looked at my wife and said, "I'm headed to the swamp." On my way to the swamp, I knocked on Rob's door and he looked up from his easy chair, smiled, and motioned for me to come in. I told Rob that my daddy died and I was headed to the swamp. He asked, "Anything I can do for you?" I said, "No sir." Rob smiled and said, "Go get you some swamp yoga, boy."

I walked around to the back of the house and remembered the day after Rob died. I was headed to the swamp when I saw Rob's two brothers at his house. I asked them what I was supposed to do now that Rob was dead and they said I had been a good friend to their brother, keep doing what I do. They handed me a mason jar of holy water and a framed picture of my oldest son with his first deer.

The sound of my boys down in the woods only brought me back to reality. As I drove down into the woods I thought about that morning that I stopped by the hospital to see Rob where he was recovering from a fall in his house. There was a doctor standing over Rob and when I entered the room he asked, "Are you family?" I said, "No, just his friend." The doctor asked me to wait outside. A few minutes went by, the doctor came out and said, "Your friend said I could tell you what is going on." The doctor said, "Your friend is very sick and he is dying." I said, "He fell and broke some bones and now he is dying?" The doctor said, "With his diabetes and other complications..." and then I just tuned the doctor out. I walked into the hospital room and walked up to Rob's bed, grabbed his old skinny, cold hand, and said, "What can I do for you?" He said, "Nothing I'm just tired." A few days later, Rob was dead.

The day of the funeral, I sat in the church and listened to what they had to say about him. They talked about his time in the military and working for my old outfit, but there was no mention of the man I knew. There was no mention of how he had retired early, after his father died, so he could come home to run the family farm, when he had no intentions of being retired here. On our many talks, it was always about living out west, and how a place out there brought him peace. Later that evening, I went to the Pearl pond and shot at Rob's range by the headlights of my Jeep, saying goodbye to my friend.

As I drove up to my boys, I wiped the tears from my eyes. My boys were all smiles; children have a way of healing some of our wounds or at least temporarily. My oldest son looked at me and asked, "Daddy you ok?" I replied, "I'm fine baby, I just miss Uncle Rob."

Rob's brother has retired to the farm with his wife. They asked me the other day to teach their two grandsons how to shoot a bb gun. I know Rob would want that. Since the bb gun lesson was a success, they asked me to teach them how to drive a tractor, and I did. I wanted to take them down to the Pearl pond and show them the little plaque I made about Rob. I wanted to teach them about Uncle Rob, what he did for his country, and this piece of land, but maybe next time. I do not see them a lot, but I cannot say that is not on purpose. I have a little of Rob in me too.

Rob's other brother comes to visit and stays in Rob's house. I have grown to respect him. He is a Marine and a little rough around the edges, but he understands me. Most people stop trying to get me and just call me different. We talk on the phone often, and I can tell, like me, he has not found peace with Rob's death.

It's 6 a.m. and I'm headed to the swamp. I just drove by Rob's house, the light by his easy chair is still not on and his diesel truck is not under the carport. I parked my Jeep and eased my way into the swamp. The weather is cool so the cottonmouths are not an issue today. My deer stand is strapped to a tree twenty feet in the air. I have a very small seat and platform up there. The ground under me is not manicured or fertilized and this place lacks the influence of man. In the distance, I can hear the creek running and a hawk lands a few trees over as the sun is coming up. The hawk squeals a couple of times to let me know I am a visitor here. The part of me that is American Indian hopes that Rob came back as a hawk and is free of those images that haunted him. The other part of me hopes that, wherever Rob is, people just understand that he is not different. He simply had some bad things happen to him, that none of us can ever be prepared for, and there was no one there to help him sort through it.

No matter how many trips to the swamp, no matter how many times I place a turkey feather and pine cone next to Rob's gravesite or no matter how many times I shoot at the Pearl pond, I cannot find peace with Rob's death. I also have thought that maybe the reason I cannot find peace with his death is because there was something that I could have done to help Rob come to terms with those things he did and saw. Could I have turned those pages of his life that haunted him? Those pages that caused him to build walls and put up gates. Did I miss something or did I do what I was supposed to do, which was, be his friend?

I sit here on my perch and look down at my rubber boots. I no longer wear corrective shoes and have been known to wear cowboy boots. The swamp brought me peace after my dad died so I will keep coming back here in search of peace for Rob's death and the swamp will continue to remind me that I am just a guest.

Five years ago I met a doctor of the mind because I was doing a research project. I had no idea what peer support was or why I would need it. Throughout my whole life, if something bothered me I would go to the woods or write about it. I never cared if anyone read it, but it just felt good to put my emotions into words. The doctor and his daughters have now been to my beloved swamp. I can't say I've ever seen people use that much bug spray, but my boys and I got a good laugh out of it. I doubt the doctor internalized that me taking him into the swamp was taking him to the core of how I process. He has also shown me how we all process differently and why peer support is needed for those who have no idea how to process or how their way of processing destroys them. The doctor says I write to process, he calls it journaling. I would agree that sometimes I write to process the pages that people like Rob and I get stuck in, but in this case I think I wrote this story to tell the story of my friend Rob; the guy who lived back in the woods and was different.

My father referred to life away from our small farm as the concrete jungle. Now I find myself traveling to parts of the concrete jungle to hear the stories of men and women who get stuck on a page in their life. Some stories are worse than Rob's and some are less, but no matter what, these are pages, and sometimes chapters in a person's life where they get stuck. As the plane wheels squeal as I return home, I think about going to the swamp to find my peace. I may not have been able to help Rob turn the pages on the images that haunted him, but he has given me a place to turn the pages from the stories I hear. I'm not sure who makes the determination of who is different and who is normal, but if being different means to serve your country and change your life's plans in order to do the right thing then I'm also good with being different. Rob impacted my life and my family's life. His choice to do the right thing has helped me impact others. As I follow this road of peer support, I always see Rob ahead of me. He was my first teacher of emotional pain and what that pain can do to a person's life. His teachings, in our frequent private talks, taught me that pain resurfaces no matter how hard we try to bury it. I watched my father suffer for years from cancer and I was able to help him with his physical limitations, but with Rob all I could do was let him dictate what he wanted, which was not much. As I travel into concrete jungles I see people like Rob who do not want to burden me with the pages in their lives that they cannot turn. I never told Rob that his story was not a burden, but an honor that he thought enough of me to share the things that kept him awake at night.

The hawk just gave me one last squeal as he flew off his limb in the direction of the Pearl pond. I said under my breath, "Enjoy your day, Rob. I hope those pages that haunted you stayed in this world with me, your swamp yoga friend. I hope that maybe one day I will find peace with your death."

–WLV –

Crisis Concepts and Precepts

Lesson 13
"Doing Our Best"

It can be difficult to help someone on occasion because that person will not tell us what he needs or what he wants. An individual's unwillingness to tell someone else about pain and distress, confusion and hurt may be deliberate resistance. It could be based in pride, denial, fear, or shame. Sometimes people are ill informed and their ignorance of what happens to a human being as a result of an exposure to a traumatic experience can cause them to feel that they are weak, abnormal, or just different than other people. A hard exterior may then be developed by the traumatized person to protect him from contact with others. No one can then get through the walls that the person erects to protect himself. That type of evasiveness and the resistance to assistance can be highly disruptive to a person's healing process. An individual may know where they would like to go, but they choose the wrong way to get to their goal. Unfortunately, the person thinks that they are doing his or her best to recover, but they do not grasp that the path they have selected does not lead them to the desired recovery. There are other paths that would work better, if only they would allow someone to help develop the *roadmap*.

A person may not actually know what he or she wants or needs, so they do not know how to tell another what can be done to help them. It is possible that a person may not even know that they have sustained damage from a trauma they experienced. Again, the roadmap is missing. No expectations have been set and there are no guidelines for managing the times when their worlds have collided. The *Collision of Worlds* occurs when work bangs into private life or when childhood and adulthood experiences brush up against each other. When that collision of our separate worlds is not understood, a person may climb onto their own personal *hamster wheel*. They begin going round and round trying to figure things out, but never reaching satisfaction.

As the story "Pearl Pond" demonstrates, *triggers* remind us of many thoughts, feelings, conversations, events, and experiences from the past. Josey (WLV), the author of the story provides a rich supply of triggers that cause him to remember his friend Rob.

Important concepts: 1) Roadmap, 2) Collision of Worlds, 3) Hamster Wheel, and 4) Triggers

The concepts *Roadmap, Collision of Worlds, Hamster Wheel and Triggers* are subtlety presented in the Pearl Pond story. They are also described in plain language in separate sections earlier in this book. It may help the reader to find these sections in the table of contents and review those readings. The terms are not formal psychological terms, but these concepts have proven to be of enormous assistance to people who are struggling to understand and overcome their traumatic stress. They simplify the, sometimes complex, terminology of trauma.

We have used *Roadmap, Colliding Worlds, Hamster Wheel and Triggers* at stress and trauma conferences. Many people approach us and tell us that the terms really helped to clarify their traumatic experiences and the reactions they are now struggling through. It is as if a light came on for them. They suddenly grasped an understanding of their situation that they previously lacked. They say, "Yes, I get it now. I never understood it before, but my worlds did collide. That is why I feel so bad over this thing. Thanks." From understanding springs hope for a resolution of their distress.

Trauma, Grief and Complexity

Trauma is a significant shock to our system, typically from a sudden and unexpected source. It can generate horror, fear, anxiety, disorientation, uncertainty, and powerful feelings of distress. People will do their best to resolve and recover from a traumatic experience. Sometimes they will be successful on their own and, at other times, they will need peer or professional assistance as described in this book.

Grief is the manifestation of loss and mourning. Grief is characterized by sadness, confusion, feeling lost, crying, and seeking out places and things associated with the deceased and longing for the missing person. Grief is a very individual experience. The deeper the bonds between the deceased person and those who loved that person, the longer it will take before the loved ones adapt to the loss and appreciate deeply the legacy that the loved one has left for them. They will then feel more confident in their movement forward. In reality, however, there will always be a feeling of emptiness in one's heart for the person who died. It will most likely last a lifetime. That is normal as long as it does not disable us. Instead the lives of the people we cared about should continue to inspire us and guide us and lead us to greater accomplishments than we would have achieved without those special people in our lives.

Note: When grief is caused by a traumatic loss such as when a person dies suddenly as a result of an accident, or violence, or a disaster, the grief is more complex. That is, it takes much longer to process the loss and complete the mourning process. Traumatic grief is so complex it can cause major disruptions to a person's life and it may even generate physical problems. It is recommended that person seek professional help if they are not coping well with a traumatic loss.

Chapter 14

Touched My Heart

I awoke to a very pretty flight attendant leaning over me a few inches from my chest. I don't remember rolling down the runway or the liftoff into the sky. I missed the drink and snack service entirely. I had been dead to the world. When you are awakened from a deep sleep by a flight attendant, it sort of makes you concerned for your welfare. You think you should take your own pulse to see if you are okay. I thought, 'Is there something going on here that I should know about?'

She saw that I was awake. She said with a soft, gentle voice in a southern accent, "I am so sorry, Sir, I did not mean to wake you. I was just reading you shirt. My airline has a team that goes by a similar name." The shirt had the logo of the International Critical Incident Stress Foundation on it. I had just completed a meeting at a conference in which people who knew nothing about my work were questioning its effectiveness. It was a long, tedious meeting with people who went by the motto, "*Do not Confuse me with facts, I have already made up my mind.*" That was the reason for my fatigue.

I answered her, "Is the name of the team within your airline, 'Critical Incident Response Team'?" She answered that it was. Then she said, "I used it twice in two weeks. Isn't that amazing." I asked her what had happened that she came in

145

contact with the team twice in two weeks. She told me that there were two different situations. I asked if she cared to explain them to me.

She told me that the first situation was a man on board a flight who had a heart attack during the flight. She asked a flight attendant to tell the captain while she began Cardio Pulmonary Resuscitation (CPR). The pilot made the decision to go to the closest airport and alerted the tower that the aircraft had a medical emergency on board. The flight attendant and a medically trained passenger conducted CPR all the way to the ground and until the ambulance crew came on board and relieved them. The flight attendant said that it was the first time she had ever performed CPR. She completed the story by stating that three flight attendants came on board the aircraft. Two of them told her that they were with the Critical Incident Response Team (CIRT). The third was a replacement flight attendant who would take over her duties for the completion of the flight. The flight attendant who had performed CPR on the man left with the two CIRT personnel.

They sat with her and asked if she would like to tell the story. She did so in great detail. They took her to dinner and then got her settled into a hotel for the evening. She said it was great to have two people take care of her when she was upset about the CPR case. It was especially helpful when the news came that the man had not survived.

She then said "It is hard to believe, but I was on the same flight two weeks later. A baby choked on food and stopped breathing. I grabbed the baby and did one of those Heimlich maneuvers. It worked to get the food out, but the baby did not start to breathe again. So, I did mouth to mouth. The baby choked and started to breathe and I kept holding the baby and checking to see if it was breathing. We did an emergency landing in the same city where we went two weeks earlier. It is amazing, but the same two people from the CIRT program showed up. Can you believe that? Just like the last time, I was relieved from the flight and taken to a room where I could talk. Then they took me to dinner and got me into a hotel. They called in the morning to see if I was okay. They really helped me a lot."

I acknowledged that those stories represented a series of bad situations for her. I asked how she was now and she said she was fine and appreciated what the CIRT people did for her. She asked me what I did for a living. I told her what my job was about and then said, "I trained your team." She looked at my eyes and said, "Well, Sir, then you have touched my heart and I thank you for it."

– JTM –

Crisis Concepts and Precepts

Lesson 14
"Appreciation"

The vast majority of people who receive crisis intervention support services appreciate the efforts made on their behalf. They are thankful that someone made efforts to help them. They are grateful that someone listened, provided food and fluids, kept them warm, provided companionship. Sometimes people do not have to do anything special. Being present can be enough.

Once I stood in the rain next to a firefighter whose firefighter buddy was missing in the debris pile in a burned out building. I asked if there was something I could do for him. He said no. I asked if he wanted to talk. He said no. I went silent and stood with him for nearly an hour. We did not say a word to each other. Then they found the body of his firefighter buddy. When the body was carefully and honorably removed from the scene, the firefighter turned to me and shook my hand. He said, "Thank you for your kindness." I said, "I am so sorry that your friend died." He said, "I appreciate that" and walked away toward his unit.

When we support others, we sometimes have to be active. Sometimes we have to try to get people talking. Other times we stay silent. On occasion, someone will thank us for our efforts. There are times that nothing we do or say can make any difference. Thanks may be absent in some situations, but in your heart, you will know that you made a difference. "Thanks", "no thanks" does not really matter a great deal. Listen to your heart. It will usually tell you if you made a difference in a crucial moment.

Being present in the moment is what is really necessary. Sometimes, we just have to show up.

Chapter 15

A Prayer for Susan

I left the bank grateful that I had a check for the proper amount of funds to put toward the down payment and other fees and expenses on our new home. It had been an upsetting week of bank errors, poor communications from the builder, misinformation about the settlement date and procedures, a false start toward settlement and a delay in the transfer of funds from an investment firm to the bank. I clutched the check, happy that the endurance was coming to an end.

I was preoccupied with so many items and issues that my brain was working overtime just to keep an inventory of everything I was trying to process. There was the unexpected separation and the unwanted divorce. The legal expenses were an enormous burden. The cost of moving everything into storage and then paying to move it again to the new house was huge. There was credit card debt and loans from relatives. There was the unhappiness of my two girls who didn't want divorced parents and who clearly did not like apartment living. The list went on and on. I was pleased for a check in hand and the new home, but overwhelmed by being essentially broke and uncertain about the future. I was just trying to keep my head up for the sake of my girls, but I was at one of the lowest parts of my life.

I was so distracted and so deep in thought that I barely noticed the man get out of the white pick-up truck with the ladders on a rack over the bed. He had backed it into the space next to mine. Awfully close to my vehicle, I thought. He walked a few steps toward the bank. Then he quickly turned and came back toward me as I reached my truck. He said something toward my direction. His face looked quite strained. I wasn't sure if was anger or anguish. I was startled. I saw his mouth move again, but I could not hear him. I said, "Excuse me?" Now my brain went on high alert. He spoke again, but I could not understand what he was saying. Is this a robbery? Is he going to hurt me? Am I under some form of attack? Is there an accomplice? Should I run? I had already unlocked the doors of my truck with the key fob. I opened the driver's side a little and threw the envelope with the check inside and relocked the door and quickly closed it. I could not get in easily. His truck was too close to mine. I moved toward him. He was very close to me now. I braced for a possible altercation. I said, "Sir, I am sorry but I am having a hard time hearing you."

"Are you a prayerful man?" He bit his lower lip. His chin was trembling. I was still scanning for a weapon, but his hands were in plain sight. No weapon. I wasn't sure if I had heard him correctly. I said, "Sir, did you ask if I am a prayerful man?" He said, a little louder this time, "Yes. Are you a prayerful person?"

I responded, "Yes, Sir, I am. What's happening?" He began to cry. Part of me was concerned that this might be a scam. Another part was bursting with sympathy for this stranger. He then blurted out through his sobs, "My oldest girl got in with the wrong crowd. She got hooked on heroine. I am afraid she will die if she doesn't get the right help soon. She is 19 years old. I don't want her to die. Can you please say a prayer for her? Her name is Susan. She really needs some prayers. Would you say a prayer for my Susan?"

I offered my hand and he grasped it. I put a hand on his shoulder. "Yes, Sir, I will say a prayer for your Susan." He said, "Thank you, Sir, you are so kind." He turned quickly and got in his truck, started it and drove away. I was trying to figure out what else I should do, but he was gone. No markings on the truck. All white. License plate rusted and banged up. I don't' think I could have read it in any case. Blurred vision (from excess fluid in my eyes). I have rarely been so confused.

My issues suddenly did not seem so overwhelming. Deeply touched by his plea, I got in my truck and cried for this concerned father and his daughter in trouble. I said a prayer for Susan.

– JTM –

Crisis Concepts and Precepts

Lesson 15
"Crucial Moments Are Not Rare"

Crucial moments are everywhere. There is no shortage of people who are hurting for a myriad of reasons. The world is filled with people who have losses, threats, unhealed wounds, overwhelming emotions and who have just witnessed or been through too much. Everywhere there are people like Phil, Norris, Stephen, Rob, and Susan. There are worried moms and dads and brothers and sisters, friends, colleagues and neighbors, and complete strangers who need us during a crucial moment. There will be times when each human being (including the helpers among us) will need someone to help them through some crucial moments in time.

We just have to be alert to the crucial moments that come our way and respond in the moment. Sometimes we will have time to think and plan and prepare. Our efforts will mostly be effective. Other crucial moments will arise and without a plan and barely a thought we will have to do something. The outcomes may not be clear, but the need for action will be obvious. What we do in a twinkling of an eye may have profound effects on the people we contact or even on our own lives.

Crucial moments are opportunities for change. A "yes" or a "no" may make all the difference in the world. A hesitation or the failure to interpret the crucial moment may let it slip by us and we will never know what might have been.

Crucial moments demand that we are attentive to people and circumstances around us. Crucial moments require sometimes split-second decisions. Since results are never guaranteed, crucial moments force us to take a stand; to be our best selves and, mostly, to be courageous.

Suggested Readings

Adler, A., Litz, B., Castro, C. A., Suvak, M., Thomas, J. L., Burrell, L., . . . Bliese, P. D. (2008). A group randomized trial of critical incident stress debriefing provided to U.S. peacekeepers. *Journal of Traumatic Stress,* 21(3), 253-263.

American Psychiatric Association Committee on Civil Defense (1954). Psychological first aid in community disasters. *Journal of the American Medical Association (JAMA),* 156 (1), 36-41.)

American Psychiatric Association (1964). *First aid for psychological reactions in disasters.* Washington, DC: American Psychiatric Association.

Appel, J. W., Beebe, G. W., & Hilgardner, D.W. (1946). Comparative incidence of neuropsychiatric casualties in World War I and World War II. *American Journal of Psychiatry, 102,* 196-199.

Artiss, K. (1963). Human behavior under stress: From combat to social psychiatry. *Military Medicine,* 128, 1011-1015.

Boscarino, J. A., Adams, R. E. & Figley, C. R. (2005). A prospective cohort study of the effectiveness of employer-sponsored crisis interventions after a major disaster. *International Journal of Emergency Mental Health,* 7(1), 31-44

Breslau, N., Davis, G. C., & Andreski, P. (1991). Traumatic events and post-traumatic stress disorder in an urban population of young adults. *Archives of General Psychiatry, 48,* 216-222.

Breznitz, S. (1980). Stress in Israel. In. H. Selye (Ed.) *Selye's Guide to Stress Research.* (pp.71-89). New York: Van Nostrand Reinhold Co.

Brown, M. W., & Willliams, F. E. (1918). *Neuropsychiatry and the war: A bibliography with abstracts.* New York: National Committee for Mental Hygiene.

Caplan, G. (1961). *An approach to community mental health.* New York: Grune and Stratton.

Caplan, G. (1964). *Principles of Preventive Psychiatry.* New York: Basic Books.

Carkhuff, R., & Traux C. (1965). Lay mental health counseling. *Journal of Consulting Psychology, 29,* 426-431.

Deahl, M., Srinivasan, M., Jones, N., Thomas, J., Neblett, C., & Jolly, A. (2000). Preventing psychological trauma in soldiers: The role of operational stress training and psychological debriefing. *British Journal of Medical Psychology, 73,* 77-85.

Everly, G. (1989). *A clinical guide to the treatment of the human stress response.* New York: Plenum Press.

Glass, A. J. (1954). Psychological first aid in community disaster. *Journal of the American Medical Association, JAMA,* 156 (1), 36-41)

Kobassa, S.C. (1979). Stressful life events, personality, and health: An inquiry into hardiness. *Journal of Personality and Social Psychology, 37,* 1-11.

Kobassa, S.C., Maddi, S.R., & Kahn, S. (1982). Hardiness and health: a prospective study. *Journal of Personality and Social Psychology,* 42, 168-177.

Herman, J. L. (1992). Complex PTSD. *Journal of Traumatic Stress, 5,* 377-392.

Lazarus, R.S. (1966). *Psychological Stress And The Coping Process.* New York: McGraw-Hill

Lazarus, R. S. (1969). *Patterns of adjustment and human effectiveness.* New York: McGraw-Hill.

Lifton, R.J. (1970). *History and human survival: Essays on the young and the old, survivors and the dead, peace and war, and on contemporary psychohistory.* New York: Random House.

Lifton, R. J. (1973). *Home from the War: Vietnam Veterans—Neither Victims nor Executioners.* New York: Simon & Schuster.

Lifton R. J. (1993). *The protean self: Human resilience in an age of fragmentation,* New York: Basic Books.

Mitchell, J. T., & Resnik, H. L. P. (1986). *Emergency response to crisis.* Ellicott City, MD: Chevron Publishing (reprinted from original, 1981).

Mitchell, J. T. (1983). When disaster strikes...The critical incident stress debriefing process. *Journal of Emergency Medical Services, 8,* 36-39.

Mitchell, J. T. (1988a). History, status and future of CISD. *Journal of Emergency Medical Services, 13,* 49-52.

Mitchell, J. T. (1988b). Development and functions of a critical incident stress debriefing team. *Journal of Emergency Medical Services, 13,* 43-46.

Mitchell, J. T. (1991). Law enforcement applications of critical incident stress debriefing teams. In J. T. Reese (Ed.), *Critical Incidents in Policing* (pp. 289-302). Washington, DC: U.S. Department of Justice.

Mitchell, J. T. (2007). *Group crisis support: Why it works, when and how to provide it.* Ellicott City, MD: Chevron Publishing.

Mitchell, J. T. (2013). *Care and feeding of a successful critical incident management team.* Ellicott City, MD: Chevron Publishing.

Mitchell, J. T., & Everly, G. S. (2001). *Critical incident stress debriefing: An operations manual for CISD, defusing and other group crisis intervention services* (3rd ed.). Ellicott City, Maryland: Chevron Publishing.

Paturel, A. (November 2012). Power in numbers. *Monitor on Psychology,* pp 48, 49

Pennebaker, J., & Susman, J. (1988). Disclosure of traumas and psychosomatic processes. *Social Science, and Medicine, 26,* 327-332.

Roberts, A. (2005). Bridging the past and present to the future of crisis intervention and crisis management. In Allen Roberts (Ed.) *Crisis Intervention Handbook: Assessment, Treatment and Research. Third Edition.* New York: Oxford University Press.

Salmon, T. W. (1919). War neuroses and their lesson. *New York Medical Journal, 109,* 993- 994.

Solomon, Z., and Benbenishty, R. (1986). The role of proximity, immediacy, and expectancy in frontline treatment of combat stress reaction among Israelis in the Lebanon War. *American Journal of Psychiatry,* 143, 613-617.

Stierlin, E. (1909) *Psycho-neuropathology as a result of a mining disaster March 10, 1906.* Zurich: University of Zurich.

van der Hart, O., Brown, P., & van der Kolk, B. (1989). Pierre Janet's treatment of post-traumatic stress. *Journal of Traumatic Stress, 2,* 379-396.

Vogt, J., Leonhardt, J., Koper, B. &Pennig, S. (2004). Economic evaluation of CISM – A pilot study. *International Journal of Emergency Mental Health,* 6(4), 185-196.

Yalom, I. (1985). *Theory and Practice of Group Psychotherapy* (3rd ed.). New York: Basic Books

21877418R00097

Made in the USA
Middletown, DE
14 July 2015